NATHAN HODGE

THE ART
AND CRAFT
OF CHOCOLATE

AN ENTHUSIAST'S GUIDE TO SELECTING, PREPARING, AND
ENJOYING ARTISAN CHOCOLATE AT HOME

QUARRY

Brimming with creative inspiration, how-to projects, and useful information to enrich your everyday life, Quarto Knows is a favorite destination for those pursuing their interests and passions. Visit our site and dig deeper with our books into your area of interest: Quarto Creates, Quarto Cooks, Quarto Homes, Quarto Lives, Quarto Drives, Quarto Explores, Quarto Gifts, or Quarto Kids.

First Published in 2018 by Quarry Books, an imprint of The Quarto Group, 100 Cummings Center, Suite 265-D, Beverly, MA 01915, USA.
T (978) 282-9590 F (978) 283-2742 QuartoKnows.com

Quarry Books titles are also available at discount for retail, wholesale, promotional, and bulk purchase. For details, contact the Special Sales Manager by email at specialsales@quarto.com or by mail at The Quarto Group, Attn: Special Sales Manager, 401 Second Avenue North, Suite 310, Minneapolis, MN 55401, USA.

10 9 8 7 6 5 4 3 2 1

ISBN: 978-1-63159-466-3

Digital edition published in 2018

eISBN: 978-1-63159-467-0

Library of Congress Cataloging-in-Publication Data available

Cover Image: Mike Grippi
Cover and page design: Laura Klynstra
Photography: Mike Grippi, www.mikegrippi.com
Illustration: Courtesy of Rakka Choclate

Printed in China

THIS BOOK IS DEDICATED TO

my grandparents, Lyle and Marian Wolf,

and Ray and Betty Hodge,

who taught me in words and actions

about the importance of hard work and generosity.

CONTENTS

FOREWORD

I am looking up, way up, into the thinning branches of the rainforest's upper canopy. Barely discernable is a leaf-blurred blotch of grey. What I am looking at, my companion assures me, is a sloth. I squint for all I'm worth. Meanwhile, giant peacock-blue butterflies flop through the leaves. The belligerent scream of a mantled howler monkey echoes from the shadows. A pleasant sensation envelopes my feet as I sink deeper and deeper into the crimson mud squeezing up around my boots. The air is a warm squash soup that swirls sluggishly over us.

From out of nowhere a smile of radiant Mayan gold teeth greets us, a Cheshire cat disguised as a farmer wearing rubber galoshes over baggy pants and a sweat-drenched long-sleeved shirt. He leads us to what might generously be called a hut—essentially a roof of thatch erected over an old wood-burning stove, with a spring-fed spigot pouring continuously into a tin tub, overflowing, and eroding a small canyon through the dirt floor. I splash cold water on my face, but when I begin to drink from cupped hands, the farmer whips out his machete. Faster than you can say *que demonios*, he hacks open fresh coconuts for each of us to drink. "Gracias," I say, and glance at the pile of football-shaped pods resting on the cold iron of the stove. Again the flash of a machete, and I'm handed half a red-yellow-green pod that's filled with a goop of slimy white seeds. I pop one in my mouth.

And it hits me—something like a neutron bomb of kiwi, mango, passion fruit, tangerine, and cranberry-pomegranate Emergen-C.

My first experience with raw cacao revealed to me the enormous gulf between what we know we don't know, and what we don't know we don't know. The presumption that my lifelong penchant for devouring chocolate bars would somehow prepare me for tasting the raw material of chocolate was so naïve it bordered on arrogant. This tension between presumption and truth, comfort and exhilaration, strangeness and connection fuels many people's interest in food in general, but nowhere is it more keenly felt than in chocolate.

It was the promise of this enduring tension that inspired the opening in 2006 of my shop, The Meadow, in a sunny corner of a courtyard in an untraveled pocket of Portland, Oregon. We chose reclaimed old-growth Douglas fir and cedar for the shelves because, hard as it is to imagine now, back then it was the most inexpensive material for building a shop. But the shelves had a vibration, a resonance, and they seemed to tolerate only authentic and beautiful products.

Rather than sell confections like truffles, we decided to focus on chocolate bars. But which bars to carry?

The first arrival was Claudio Corallo. Claudio was legit in the extreme. The story of how he became a chocolate maker was the usual one. He had taken flight from Zaire (a turbulent land now called the Democratic Republic of Congo) where he was growing coffee in such a remote location that he not only had to take a boat to get there, he had to make the boat. Stripped of his plantation and seeking a new opportunity, he found himself on a small equatorial island off the west coast of Africa called São Tomé and Príncipe. There he discovered spectacular strains of cacao languishing under a tarnished reputation and a decayed agricultural infrastructure. Employing a series of innovations in post-harvest processing—especially in fermentation—he created a chocolate that to this day stands alone.

Next to the shelves came favorites from France like the Bonnat, Pralus, Cluizel, and Valrhona. Then Italian makers, like Domori, De Bondt, Venchi, and Bonajuto, who were for some reason trickier to procure. A few kooky outliers like Zotter added flair to the shelves. From there, finding chocolate from elsewhere in the word that could keep company with such bars was challenging, but we did have options. Pacari from Ecuador, El Rey from Venezuela, and even Santander from Colombia were exotic back then, and had the added attraction of being made in the country where the cacao was grown. My favorite of all was Grenada, made by Mott Green, who died tragically in 2013. Mott was the true swashbuckler of the chocolate world, establishing a cacao cooperative, sailing around the Caribbean in search of a salt worthy of his bars, and inventing the most brilliant solutions to the meet the innumerable challenges of making chocolate in the tropics. To this day his chocolate offers an unrivalled ratio of cost to benefit, for all involved, from the farmer to your mouth.

In the United States, we were harder pressed to find bars. Scharffen Berger was making great chocolate but their acquisition by Hershey's tempered our enthusiasm. Guittard, founded in 1868 and the oldest family-owned chocolate company in the country, was far bigger than our more boutique European chocolate makers, but like the European makers, they offered bars made from a single origin and were active in the effort to improve the economic situation of cacao growers everywhere. Luckily Taza and Theo had just opened their doors, and a few others trickled in over the course of the next year or two.

Exclusivity was a recurring theme among the more vaunted makers. Amedie ran us through an intimidating vetting process. Bernachon never answered my calls. An eccentric genius named Steve DeVries was making great chocolate in Colorado, but he turned me down flat when I approached him, asserting our curatorial process was not assiduous enough for him. He wasn't far off the mark.

I wanted to share more than just artisanship, I wanted to share experiences. Chocolate studded with toasted piedmont hazelnuts bought at a roadside market in the Alps. Coarse crystals of sugar in chocolate so rough it wouldn't melt in the stifling bullfighting rings of Santiago de Querétaro. Plus, those chocolates are delicious. So we brought in some favorites from the road: Valor from Spain, Villars from Switzerland, Weiss from France, and Hachez from Germany.

If you've never had Claudio Corallo, here's how you can recreate the flavor in the convenience of your own home:

1. Find a small box

2. Inside it, pack one medium-size jungle

3. Put the box on top of 300 kg of thermite

4. Strike a match

That should do it.

In 2006 chocolate-making was a distinctly European enterprise. But in the last decade, North America has come to rival, and in its own way even surpass, the best of Europe, with brands such as Castronovo, Fruition, Askinosie, Dick Taylor, Patric, and the fugitive Rogue. My home town of Portland seems to be an incubator for chocolate companies, with half a dozen talented makers following the likes of Woodblock and Stirs the Soul. Today there are more than 200 bean-to-bar chocolate makers in the United States alone. Hundreds more have sprung up elsewhere around the world. From Argentina's weirdly Russian-inspired Mamuschka to New Zealand's wonderfully named Hogarth—and everything in between, from Iceland's opulent Omnom to Hungary's unpronounceable scrumptious Rózsavölgyi to Japan's minimalist Minimal. There is no end to the list. What makes them special? Their very newness is certainly part of it. You can tell. Each chocolate bar harbors that flicker of excited discovery, each ultimately bonded to those crazy tangy cacao seeds.

The global phenomenon of bean-to-bar is reflected by the creative fervor inside the Raaka factory itself, where recipes reflect the full multiculturalism and dimensionality of chocolate: its origins, processes, people, tastes, attitudes, and memories. In Raaka, Nate and Ryan bring a perspective that is both adventurous and inclusive. They tell stories. Not just their stories, but the stories that each of us has bound up in our relationship to chocolate. As Nate puts it, "Everybody has nostalgia for a flavor. Let's take those flavors and make them at least grown up, if not sophisticated."

Nate is being modest. Smart reflections on flavor isn't all that Raaka is up to. As keenly as any Claudio Corallo, these folks are chasing something in the narrative arc of the bean-to-bar movement itself.

Bean-to-bar chocolate is not the first artisanal movement. Craft beer, for one, germinated from a handful of makers and blossomed into a worldwide movement. But while beer is consumed socially, chocolate has generally been viewed as a personal pleasure. Nate and Ryan see an opportunity to create something new in this distinction: a public community rooted in a love of chocolate. Looking back, it isn't hard to see that this is precisely what's going on. Eating chocolate is evolving from personal pleasure to a catalyst for social, agricultural, cultural, and even artistic awareness. Judging from the conflagration of new makers popping up everywhere, not only are artisans warming to this idea, we the chocolate eating public are, too.

Those same tensions I discovered so many years ago—the raw energy of the discovery and enjoyment and human connection—are captured in full color in these pages. So whether you are a farmer in the tropics or a consumer somewhere else, bean-to-bar chocolate invites you to join a community where the yearning to live in harmony is not just an ideal, it is a tangible objective measured in increments of deliciousness.

MARK BITTERMAN
CEO and Selmelier
The Meadow
November 14, 2017

INTRODUCTION

My first experience with making chocolate went poorly. It was the fall of 2009, and I was living in Somerville, Massachusetts. The square near my apartment had a lovely weekday afternoon farmers' market. On one October afternoon, a booth I had frequented a few times to buy Taza Chocolate had cocoa beans for sale. I had recently roasted coffee beans in my oven at home, and I really enjoyed how they turned out, so I jumped at the chance to buy cocoa beans and roast them. These beans came in a cool miniature burlap sack, but they also came with no instructions. I didn't think I needed instructions, because at this point I was a pro at roasting coffee. How much different could roasting cocoa beans be?

That weekend I fired up my oven to 450°F (230°C), because that's what I had roasted my coffee at. When the oven had preheated, I arranged my beans on a baking tray and put it in the oven. Very quickly, the kitchen began to smell like brownies, and I was pleased. After six or seven minutes, though, the smell began to change to a distinctly burnt smell, and smoke began to seep out my oven door. I turned off the oven and opened it. I immediately heard a series of small pops, and then my cocoa beans burst into flames. After this incident, I did some research and found out that I had roasted my cocoa beans at least 125°F (52°C) too hot.

When I met Ryan Cheney in New York City a year later, his concept for Raaka was appealing to me: "We're gonna make chocolate bars without roasting the cocoa beans." Great, I thought, I can dive deep into learning how to make chocolate, but I won't have to deal with another cocoa bean fire.

The appeal was obviously about more than just fire prevention. Raw cocoa beans have interesting and intense flavors that are developed during post-harvest fermentation. These flavors are also aided by the different terroirs in which they're grown. Cocoa beans grown on the arid coast of northern Peru taste completely different from cocoa beans grown beneath the cloud forests in the valleys of the Sierra de Chama mountains in central Guatemala. In the mostly mass-scale chocolate I had been exposed to, Taza being the lone exception, these flavors were completely stripped of their nuance through heavy roasting and processing. Raaka has always been interested in making the difference in these flavors abundantly clear to customers and collaborators. In my own personal experience with chocolate, I was so far removed from knowing anything about where chocolate came from, how it was made, and what the agricultural product that chocolate originates from even looks like that tasting the raw beans was revelatory.

When I began to discuss chocolate with my family and friends, I quickly found that the story of chocolate wasn't revelatory just to me. It turned out that chocolate was full of mystery to everyone I knew.

Humans have been consuming the stuff for at least 3,000 years, and in recent history, we've become far removed from its origins and the globetrotting essence it embodies. I've been all over the world and connected with people far different from me because of the one thing we had in common: chocolate. Chocolate unites people because it makes everyone happy. Its mysterious mix of unique alkaloids allows it to do this. At Raaka, whether it's the farmers we buy from, the many companies we collaborate with, our employees, or our customers, we just want to make the world a happier, more equitable place. I acknowledge that it's a cheesy and simple goal, but it's one we're going to defend, because what other goal fits with something as joy-inducing as chocolate?

Raaka is influenced by the city we operate in: New York. Our city is full of multiple cultures all mashing together and attempting to live in balance and harmony. It gives New York an energy that not all cities have. Our bars have always been inspired by the many flavors and ingredients that can be found all over the city. Every culture is represented here. If there's a dish you enjoy from some far-off corner of the globe, chances are there's a tiny restaurant in Queens where you can find it. The culinary energy of the city drives our desire for constant experimentation. In the past seven years, we've made over 200 different flavors of chocolate. These flavors have been influenced by everything from Thai soups to Mexican beverages to Indian spices. I have no doubt that the creativity that pumps through the fabric of Raaka comes from being in the mecca for cuisine in the United States. New York fuels us.

This book is an attempt to share that creativity and love of culture with you. Let's begin to look beyond chocolate as the stuffy bonbon or truffle you give as a gift only on special occasions. Chocolate is a food that unites, excites, and inspires with the many mysteries of its history and raw materials. This book is an exploration of those mysteries. Along the way, we'll encounter some tips for making chocolate at home, and we'll make some food using chocolate as the star ingredient. Don't worry—we'll always think about safety first.

INTRODUCTION OF TERMS

Before we dive into where chocolate really comes from, let's lay out some basic terms to avoid confusion. The truth is, the cacao tree contains many by-products that we will discuss, and without setting the scene in terms of what is what, I run the risk of confusing you. Consider the following your guide to the wonders that are the by-products of the cacao tree.

CACAO POD: This is the fruit of the cacao tree. It manifests itself in the form of a pod, which can range from the size of a fist to the size of a football. Cacao pods generally contain 25 to 50 seeds. The color of these pods can be purple, yellow, red, green, orange, or anything in between.

CACAO PULP: This is a sticky white mucilage surrounding the seeds that is the sweet, edible fruit part of the cacao pod. Cacao fruit is needed for the fermentation process that turns cacao seeds into cocoa beans. Its taste can be both sweet and tart, and can range in flavor from green apple to cantaloupe to vanilla pudding.

CACAO SEEDS: These are the purple seeds that sit in the white pulp of the cacao pod. They are surrounded by a fibrous outer layer, not unlike sunflower seeds. Since they are seeds and can germinate, they are referred to as cacao seeds instead of cocoa seeds.

COCOA BEANS: These are the fermented and dried cacao seeds that are, at some point, the basis for all the chocolate in the world. Since they can no longer germinate and become new cacao trees, they are referred to as cocoa beans. After they are dried, they have a tough, fibrous outer shell that needs to be removed and a dark brown inner bean that is the most desirable part of the cacao tree and the reason cacao is grown.

COCOA NIBS: These are the cracked inner portion of the cocoa bean. Cocoa nibs are made up of roughly half cocoa butter and half cocoa powder. These nibs will always be ground down using some method and are the basis for most chocolate. The percentage of a chocolate bar is the amount of that chocolate bar that is ground-up nibs. Say a chocolate bar is labeled as 70 percent dark: This means that 70 percent of its content is ground-up cocoa nibs, while the other 30 percent is sugar.

COCOA BUTTER: This is the vegetable fat that is present in the cocoa nib. It is cocoa butter's smooth, silky texture that gives chocolate its decadent mouthfeel. Cocoa butter melts at the temperature of the human body, making it extra alluring to the senses. Cocoa butter can be extracted from the cocoa nib using a press. Extracted cocoa butter is valuable in cosmetics, confections, and as a processing agent in chocolate making.

COCOA POWDER: This is the solid of the cocoa nib, the other part you get when you extract cocoa butter. Cocoa powder is where chocolate gets most of its flavor and its desirable alkaloids, caffeine and theobromine. Cocoa powder is complex, consisting of carbohydrates, minerals, alkaloids, flavonoids (antioxidants), and protein.

COCOA LIQUOR: This is not alcohol, but rather the cocoa nibs ground down into a smooth paste. Cocoa liquor is often imported and used to make chocolate products instead of starting from scratch with the beans.

PART I

A BRIEF HISTORY OF CHOCOLATE

CHAPTER 1

CHOCOLATE COMES FROM A TREE

The agricultural and culinary landscape of human existence is full of mystery; it's what has always drawn me to it. Think about the way kimchi and sauerkraut are fermented cabbage dishes that two very different cultures tens of thousands of miles away from each other discovered and used as a major source of nutrients in cold weather, or contemplate that there are 4,000 different types of potatoes native to the Andes—these are the mysteries and bits of human ingenuity that make the world of food so inspiring.

Chocolate is no different. It begins as a finicky fruit that grows only in certain climates and only within a specific belt around the equator. The cocoa bean has ancient roots in the Amazon basin and made its way up through Mesoamerica. As an agricultural product, cocoa beans' roots are deeply imbedded in the ancient practice of agroforestry. The cocoa bean itself contains many compounds and minerals that have been sought after for millennia. Getting from a fruit on a tree to a chocolate bar is a long and tedious journey, but one full of intrigue. Let's discover how a brightly colored, football-shaped pod makes its way from a flower to a seed to a chocolate bar.

WHERE DOES THE CACAO TREE GROW?

Before sumptuous melted chocolate becomes a chocolate bar, chocolate begins with a tree. The *Theobroma cacao* tree loves the tropics, absolutely loves them. If fact, this tree loves the tropics so much that it refuses to grow outside of 20 degrees north or south of the equator. Given that 70 percent of the planet is made up of water, 20 degrees north or south of the equator isn't very much of the planet. Additionally, less than 28 percent of the world's total landmass sits within this latitude. We're talking about only around 8 percent of the globe that even qualifies for growing cacao.

However, cacao also has other conditions it prefers. Cacao doesn't like to grow anywhere above 1,000 meters, and never below 65°F (18°C). Cacao needs humidity and a lot of rainfall to thrive as well. If we inspect the belt of 20 degrees north and south of the equator a little closer, we'll find half of the Andes Mountains in South America and mountain ranges and highlands in Mexico, Guatemala, India, Myanmar, Indonesia, Rwanda, the Democratic Republic of Congo, and others. In addition to mountains, we'll find about a third of the Sahara Desert, half of Australia's Gibson Desert, as well as deserts in Peru, Chile, Kenya, Ethiopia, and many arid climates elsewhere. If we add it all up, we're looking at less than 4 percent of the planet that can be a habitat for the cacao tree.

New cacao trees are planted two different ways. The first is the most traditional. A cacao seed is selected and allowed to germinate in a bag of nutrient-rich soil. After it grows to be about a foot-and-a-half tall and forms branches, it is taken from its small nutrient-rich home and placed in a new spot among the other cacao trees. Cacao trees need to be planted about 5 feet (1.5 m) apart so as not to crowd each other. The second way to grow a new cacao tree is by using parts of two older cacao trees. This method is called grafting. To graft a cacao tree, you select budwood, or a small branch, off a large branch of a productive tree. Then you slice a v-shaped cut into the base of an existing tree that is getting too large or is no longer as productive as you'd like. You insert a whittled end of the budwood into the v-shape cut of the existing tree and wrap it with plastic wrap to prevent the cut from drying out and killing your budwood. If your graft takes, the budwood you've grafted on to your existing tree should start to flourish after a few days.

Trees that are planted from seeds are often grafted as well. For getting the most possible and easy-to-reach production out of a cacao tree, it is best for the tree to bifurcate, or split into two, as close as possible to the ground. To aid in this process, seedlings, or new trees, will be grafted so that they grow out into two equal sections that feed off the tree's roots. Once a grafted branch starts to flower, in one to two years, the existing low-yielding tree is cut down so that the baby tree can spread its wings. In the third year, the tree will start to fruit, and usually by the fourth or fifth year, you'll get your first harvest from a cacao tree.

THE CACAO FLOWER AND A SMALL FLY

In addition to how finicky cacao trees are about their environment, they are also very particular about how they want to be pollinated. Cacao flowers are tiny, funny-looking white flowers that dangle off the branch of the tree ever so delicately. A strong gust of wind can send cacao flowers flying from the tree they're meant to give life to. These tiny flowers also have a tiny protective shield that hides their pollen-producing anthers. Because of this shield, the cacao tree cannot be pollinated by a bee, like a normal plant, but instead relies on a tiny fly called a midge to pollinate its flowers. Midges range from just one to three millimeters in size. To complicate things, only the flies that grow larger than two millimeters are large enough to carry the pollen. The cacao midge is related to the mosquito and biting midges are common. Their bites can be quite nasty and plentiful when they're in season.

Complicating things even further, the cacao flower only lives for about two days, and each midge can barely carry enough pollen to pollinate one flower. These complications mean that it's quite a miracle for a tree to ever fruit to begin with. Only about 1 in every 300 cacao flowers will fruit. Of those fruits, only about half of them fruits will ever come to maturity. In the twenty-year lifespan of a cacao tree, it might produce around 150,000 flowers. Only about fifteen years of that lifespan will produce well for the farmer. One cacao pod represents about one 70 percent dark chocolate bar. So that means that in its life cycle, a healthy, average cacao tree will only produce about 250 chocolate bars. To put this into perspective, my small company produces about 350,000 chocolate bars a year in addition to producing baking chocolate for restaurants. This means that if I were to grow my own cocoa beans, I would have to start with a minimum of 1,400 trees to get the amount I needed for an average year of bar production.

CACAO GENETICS

Some people will try and tell you that cacao is full of genetic diversity just like apples and grapes used to make wine. With apples you get different flavors and textures from Gala and Pink Lady, and with wine you get different flavors, colors, and mouthfeel from Pinot Noir than you do from Sauvignon Blanc. Technically, this genetic diversity exists in cacao as well. I have used this comparison to briefly explain genetic diversity before. It's a useful tool to paint a picture when it comes to describing how and why different cocoa beans taste, smell, and look different. Unfortunately, it is only really a half-truth. The whole truth is quite convoluted.

Cacao is widely talked about as having four types of genetic varieties: Forastero, Criollo, Trinitario, and Nacional. This is an oversimplification. These aren't necessarily cacao varieties as much as they are signifiers for cacao from certain regions. I'll describe what these four names represent for the purposes of context. It is almost pointless to talk about the flavor variation in these four types of cacao, and you'll see why soon.

FORASTERO: The name of this cacao comes from a Spanish word whose literal translation is "stranger." It got this name because it referenced cacao that was not native to the Spanish empire. As a result, the cacao that grew in Brazil, and later in Africa, got this name. In a general sense, this cacao is very different from the cacao grown in Peru, Guatemala, Ecuador, and so on, so the name does make some sense. However, it's become a blanket term used to describe cacao from Africa, some of which did not come from Brazil, but came from Central America or the Caribbean. There are also several different types of cacao that originate from Brazil, though they all tend to get lumped into the category of Forastero.

CRIOLLO: This is a variety of cacao native to Mesoamerica, more specifically the Yucatán and parts of Belize. Criollo is a specific genotype found in those areas. It is quite rare and very susceptible to disease, but you will find it and it

is quite special. However, *criollo* is also a slang term used in Peru to describe anything wild or potentially native to specific regions. Also, because this type of cacao generally garners a higher price, in countries all over Central America people will use this term to describe cacao that predates an individual's knowledge of their land and the crops that are grown on it. If it is originally from an old tree and looks different than the hybridized modern varieties a farmer is growing, chances are they will call it Criollo or try to sell it as Criollo. That's not to say that the strange cacao they have may or may not be special; it's just that it might not be a true Criollo.

TRINITARIO: The Spanish brought true Criollo cacao to the island of Trinidad in the seventeenth century after they realized that it couldn't be grown back home in Spain. In 1727, a hurricane destroyed most of the Criollo cacao in Trinidad. Thirty years later, the Spanish brought heartier Forastero trees from Venezuela to Trinidad. These trees were likely a slightly more specific type of cacao, *amelonado*, or "that which looks like a melon." The Forastero mixed with the remaining Criollo trees and a new type of cacao was born, the Trinitario, or "that which is from Trinidad" (sense a theme?). Trinitario was brought back to the Spanish colonies and became prevalent as the global cacao trade grew. This is what most of the cacao grown in Latin America and the Caribbean is referred to as today.

NACIONAL: A fourth type of cacao was "discovered" in Ecuador in the 1970s and called Nacional. This cacao is essentially the Criollo of Ecuador. It is a specialized cacao that is susceptible to disease, like Criollo, and only really takes hold in the rainforests in Ecuador, Colombia, and northeastern Peru. As with Criollo, anyone who has anything other than the hybrid cacaos prevalent in Ecuador is likely to refer to what they have as Nacional.

Okay, so let's unpack this a little. Not a lot of research was done concerning the genetics of cacao varietals until the twenty-first century. Even in this century, most of the research being done is being done not to solve the puzzle of cacao genetics, but to determine where the most disease-resistant varieties are and whether they have the same level of heartiness and durability in different regions and on different continents. In 2008, a paper was published naming ten different types of cacao, and since then several others have been identified, but again, we're talking about very recent history. So much is still unknown, and giant swaths of the map of Amazonia have yet to be studied and data mapped, but what we do know is that the identification of cacao types from a single farm can be very difficult.

Some cacao varieties are self-incompatible (they need pollen from a different plant) and some are self-compatible (they can pollinate with two flowers from the same tree). Grapes, on the other hand, are almost all self-compatible, while apples are self-incompatible. With grapes, unintended genetic mutations rarely occur and thus varietal purity is common and celebrated. Farmers who grow apples almost always use the pollen from a crabapple tree to pollinate the apple blossoms of the variety of apple they're trying to grow. When you manage an apple farm, you go to great lengths to ensure that your different varieties of apple groves are separated and that crabapple trees are evenly dispersed to encourage pollination with those trees. Using the crabapple maintains the relative genetic purity of the particular apple and ensures that the phenotypes (the shape, color, texture, flavor, and so forth) of that type of apple remain consistent.

This method for farming apples is generally not applied to cacao, and therefore the mixing that happens from one type of cacao to another is rarely done in a controlled manner. The world is mostly full of cacao varieties that have been haphazardly mixed over thousands of years. As cacao seeds and plants traveled up and down the Amazon, up to Central America from South America, brought to the Caribbean and over to Africa and Asia by the French, Spanish, English, Portuguese, and Dutch, the varieties got all cross-pollinated and mixed up. What you'll find on a cacao farm is beautiful: many shapes, colors, sizes, and textures of cacao pods. It's truly breathtaking, but it's a sign of confused phenotypes, and not a good indication of being able to determine simply what genetic type of cacao exists on a given farm. One of the main reasons why the separation of cacao varieties has been de-prioritized on cacao farms is because the land management of these farms can be extremely difficult.

MANAGING A CACAO FARM

Cacao is a finicky shade crop and needs a partial canopy to protect its flowers and subsequent fruits from the hot sun of the subtropics. Too much shade, however, and the *Theobroma cacao* tree can become susceptible to harmful fungus and disease. Cacao trees must be regularly pruned to ensure the leaves of the tree aren't locking in too much humidity in the grove where the trees are. This humidity can cause a fungal disease called black pod. Black pod causes the cacao fruit to rot and produce spores that can spread to other trees with the mere presence of a light breeze. The cacao tree also makes the soil it is grown in very acidic. The acidity in the soil of a cacao farm is combated by growing the cacao among trees that are nitrogen fixers. These are trees that increase the pH in the soil, causing it to even out from the acidity of the cacao tree. Limestone can also be applied to the soil around cacao trees to ensure that the acidity of the soil doesn't get too high.

Cacao pods are difficult to harvest because they need to be harvested by hand. Pods need to be cut off close to the branch, but not so close that you damage the branch, causing it to not flower during the next harvest. Cacao trees are generally kept less than 20 feet (6 m) tall to make them easier to harvest. When they grow taller than that, they need to be grafted with a productive piece of branch from a different tree at the base of the old tree. When this branch begins to mature, the old tree is cut down to right above the new branch so that its old rootstock can be used for the beginnings of the new tree.

These are the things that need to be done in addition to the normal land maintenance, like maintaining paths through the fields, raking leaves, and removing fallen branches and debris. The harvesting and processing after you get a good crop is also labor-intensive and difficult work.

HARVESTING CACAO

After cacao pods are cut from the trees, they're gathered and put into sacks. They are then carried to either a central clearing or back to a shed or dwelling where they are put in a large pile for opening. These sacks are very heavy and are carried by hand, sometimes up and down hills and for many yards at a time. When they are in a pile, they are cut down the middle with a machete, using care not to slice through any seed. When the white fruit is revealed, it is scooped out by hand with the seeds and tossed into a bucket. This mixture of wet fruit and cacao seeds is called baba. It generally takes five to seven people working two full days to harvest the cacao from a twenty-acre farm.

The buckets of baba are then carried or transported to a road where they're either loaded into a truck or placed to await the pickup of a fermentary or cooperative where they will be fermented and dried for export. The process of harvesting cacao needs to happen in a relatively short timeframe. Once cacao pods are cut from the trees, the fruit and seeds need to be removed within 5 days so that the fruit doesn't start to dry out and lose its robust sugar content. Once the fruit and seeds are removed from the pods, they need to get to a fermentary or into fermentation boxes within eight hours. This time crunch makes efficiency and an all-hands-on-deck attitude necessary for completing the job. In small rural or indigenous communities, it is common for the community to take turns harvesting each other's cacao farm over seven to ten days during the harvest season.

FERMENTING CACAO

The cacao seed is made up of knots, so to speak, of complex amino acids. The flavor of these amino acids is so strong that the human palate can only identify their flavor as intense bitterness. To break down these intense and complex knots of concentrated flavor into strands of flavor that the human senses can handle, the cacao seed needs to go through a transformation. This transformation takes place during the process of fermentation.

Cacao fermentation is a very important step in the process of making chocolate. I firmly believe that to make great chocolate, you need cocoa beans that are properly fermented. I spend most of my summer every year visiting my cacao suppliers, inspecting their fermentation facilities and monitoring their fermentation process. It is crucial to the quality of my chocolate.

The baba from the farms is brought to a fermentation facility and placed into large sweat boxes. These are wooden boxes that hold anywhere from 200 to 1,765 pounds (90 to 800 kg) of cacao. The cacao fruit is high in sugar. Natural yeasts in the air and in the wood of the boxes eat the sugars and create ethanol (alcohol). The wild yeasts also break down the pectin in the white fruit of the cacao pod and turn it into a liquid. This liquid will assist in killing the germinating part of the seed that will become the cocoa bean, and then it will drain off.

Cacao fermentation is driven by anaerobic and aerobic chemical reactions. The anaerobic reaction happens when the baba sits still in the fermentation box, allowing the sugar

Flavors of Under-Fermented and Over-Fermented Cocoa Beans

When cocoa beans are improperly fermented, they can produce some flavors or flavor characteristics that are either very tough to work with for chocolate makers or that are just plain gross to find in a chocolate bar.

Flavors of under-fermented cocoa beans:

> astringent
>
> bitter
>
> vegetal
>
> underripe grapes
>
> oversteeped tea

Flavors of over-fermented cocoa beans:

> acidic
>
> smoky
>
> oxidized wine/vinegar
>
> mushroom
>
> cheese

in the cacao fruit to turn into ethanol and later lactic acid. The aerobic reaction happens when the baba is turned from one box into another using a shovel or a bucket. When this occurs, the yeasts multiply and turn the ethanol to acetic acid. The acetic acid will permeate the shell of the cacao seed and kill its ability to germinate. After this occurs, then the flavors we associate with good chocolate can begin to form. Cacao will typically ferment for four to eight days.

During this period, the cacao may be turned from one box to another as many as five times, to strike that balance of alcohol and acetic acid that will properly break down the amino acids of the cacao seed. A little too much acetic acid, alcohol, or lactic acid and the flavor of the fermented cocoa beans can go awry. Additionally, if the baba doesn't have enough sugar or the fruit begins to drain off the seed before the fermentation can properly inoculate, the flavor of the cocoa bean can also be ruined. These two missteps are aptly referred to as over-fermentation and under-fermentation, respectively, and both can cause massive headaches for chocolate makers.

Think about it as if you were choosing fruit for a pie. The best pies are made from perfectly ripe fruit. If you choose fruit that is underripe, you're going to get a pie that is tart to

the point of unpleasantness. If you choose fruit that is past its prime, you not only risk the potential for rotten flavors in your pie, but you'll likely also have issues with the texture of your pie. When you make a fruit pie, the fruit is the star of the show, so starting with great fruit is essential. When you make good chocolate, the cocoa bean is undoubtedly the star of the show, so the quality of that ingredient is of the utmost importance, and fermentation plays the most crucial role in this.

After cocoa beans are fermented, they are still hot and sticky, and the moisture that permeated its shell is still saturated into the bean, so they need to be properly dried out.

DRYING COCOA BEANS

When they are taken out the fermentation boxes, cocoa beans are wet, sticky, and pale, and they need sunlight to dry them out and give them some color. The best way to dry out cocoa beans is to spread them out on a mesh or wooden platform or deck and rake them in the heat of the afternoon sun. This process allows any excess fruit to dry up or drain off the beans. The drying cocoa beans are raked every few hours to ensure the drying is happening evenly and to prevent mold growth. With proper sunlight and aeration, cocoa beans can dry in as few as six days. However, it is more typical that beans take between 7 and ten days to dry.

Large concrete pads are often used in the last two days to ensure the beans are fully dried. The industry standard for moisture in a cocoa bean that is ready for export is 6 to 7 percent. Large-scale commodity processors will often use mechanical driers to dry cocoa beans. These are typically large metal beds that are heated from beneath or from the side using a firebox. The advantage to this method is that the beans will dry very quickly. The disadvantage, and the reason you won't find this method implemented by producers of a quality cacao, is that this method imparts a smoky flavor to the cocoa beans. This method is useful if a cacao harvest in a given region overlaps with that region's rainy season. If the climate is wet and without sunlight, natural drying is impossible, and mechanical drying is typically used.

After cocoa beans are fermented and dried, they are put into jute sacks in quantities ranging from 110 to 155 pounds (50 to 70 kg) and stored in a warehouse. Once enough cacao has been processed and stored in the warehouse, it can be loaded into a shipping container or containers for export. Most of the world's cocoa beans are exported to Europe and the United States. With few exceptions, such as Mexico, El Salvador, Guatemala, and Brazil, most cacao-growing countries export all the cacao they produce and literally have no relationship to chocolate.

A STORY FROM
THE CACAO FIELDS

Traveling for cacao can feel very romantic; you are on dirt roads through the mountains, or on boats through the tributaries of the Amazon or across the small section of ocean that connects Belize to Guatemala. I often visit small agricultural towns where I encounter unique sights and smells from local markets. I encounter vistas and cloud forests that inspire the grandest thoughts of adventure. Cacao itself grows in lush, green sections of jungle, separate from roads and power lines, out in the wild. The ecosystem that cacao grows in is inspiring: plants, insects, animals, vines, shade crops and canopy trees, and the decay of old material becoming the fuel for growth and new life. Everything in areas of rainforest live together in harmony and conflict all at once. It truly is awe-inspiring and life-affirming.

The people I encounter inspire me to be a better person. I have been greeted countless times with wonderful meals, special chocolate drinks, gifts, or even homemade cacao wine from people who have shockingly little to their names. The generosity and warmth I've been greeted with on many a trip has been enough to restore my faith in humanity. In the Peruvian Amazon, they have a special beverage called *masato* that is served during celebrations and to guests of a village. It is considered a great honor to be served *masato* and a great insult to not imbibe. *Masato* is a drink fermented from masticated yuca—yes, yuca that's been chewed and spit out. Any cup of *masato* is certainly a memorable one, but one in particular will stand out to me for a long time.

I've traveled to a small stretch of the tributaries of the Amazon in central Peru in the Ucayali region for a few years now with a few other chocolate makers and a friend of mine whose sole focus is on land conservation as it relates to cacao.

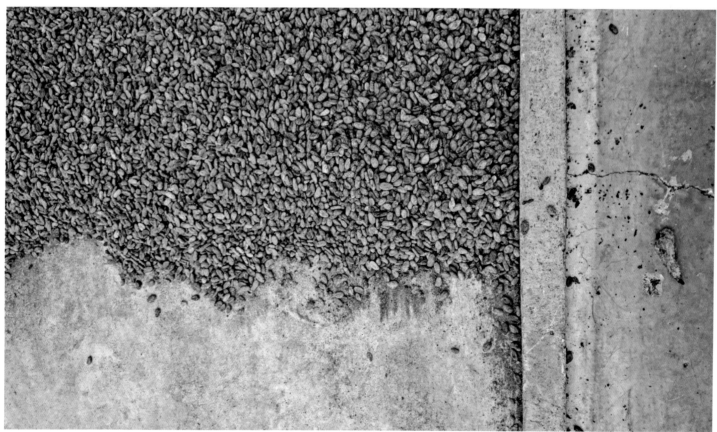

We've collected cacao samples to analyze for both flavor and genetics in a region that is essentially a blank spot on the map for cacao research.

Cacao has been growing in this section of the upper Amazon for longer than recorded human history, and we're hoping we can make a new discovery that will not only make great chocolate, but also help provide an economic stimulus to a region that has a history with civil war and a tumultuous relationship with the cocaine trade. It's a region that is absolutely gorgeous, and one of the few areas of the Amazon that's mostly untouched by global industrialization. The people of the indigenous tribes of the Ashaninka, the Machiguenga, and the Yanesha tribes load their canoes with bananas, cacao, yuca, and fish to sell in larger towns and villages. They also harvest hardwood from the jungle to sell to timber boats that travel the Amazon, but they generally live off the land, with limited access to healthcare or education.

On one particular trip, we arrived on the banks of a river at a small community that we were told by other villages had very old cacao trees that we should research. Upon arriving, we saw a few small houses and hearths, but no people, almost as if it had been abandoned. Typically in many of these small isolated communities you'll find a soccer field or a small schoolhouse, and maybe a structure that looks like a community meeting place, but in this particular community we saw none of this. We called out, but no answer.

It's not entirely uncommon for people to be out in the fields working, away from the village, but there are also commonly children or elders around in the village. There was no one here. We noticed some cacao trees, so we decided to poke around. After walking awhile through the cacao, a boy of eleven or twelve ran up to us and told us to come meet his grandfather back at one of the houses. We emerged from the cacao grove and saw a short, jolly-looking, elderly man with a bucket of *masato* and a stack of dried gourd cups. We accepted our cups of *masato*, a particularly tart batch, and proceeded to listen to him tell us his story. He told us he had been farming this particular area of land for more than fifty years. He told us that the lack of hardwood to cut down was causing many people to leave their land in search of work in larger towns. He said the river was changing, and that no young people wanted to live the life of a farmer. He lamented his lack of money, but celebrated his love for his land and the joy the forest had brought him. Then his mood shifted, and he grasped at his grandson and said, "They've all left me, my family and my friends are all gone." Tears begin to well up in his eyes as he continued, "All I have is the companionship of my grandson, and one day he'll leave me as well and I will be lonely. Then one day there will be no one here." He then held his grandson and wept. We finished our *masato* and left so that we could get back to town before nightfall. The old cacao trees he knew of, cacao de monte, had been destroyed when a larger tree fell on them during a storm.

The art and craft of chocolate making may be strong, but the craft of cacao farming is falling by the wayside. Cacao farmers live such a poor life that younger generations are leaving or being encouraged to leave to pursue a better life in more urban areas. The age of the small shareholder farmer is fast declining. When these farmers leave, their land is often swallowed up by agricultural conglomerates and used for African palm, pineapple, or cattle ranching. These three things destroy the biodiversity of the rainforest and force people and animals to flee from their habitats. Wages in cacao farming need to be increased for the very survival of indigenous ways of life and for the very survival of variety in cacao types. It's a human and an environmental problem that has no easy answers other than to chip away at the problem with small efforts from socially conscious chocolate companies, researchers, and nongovernmental organizations (NGOs). We'll talk a bit later about the problems with the price of cocoa beans.

HISTORY OF CHOCOLATE: PRE-HISPANIC MESOAMERICA

The origins of the story of chocolate remain clouded in mystery. We have archeological evidence from Mesoamerica in addition to the oral history of what the Spanish conquistadors found when they settled the New World. What we don't know is how cacao migrated to the Olmecs of the Gulf Coast, or how the Maya came to hold it in such high regard. Cacao is most likely not native to Mexico, Guatemala, or Honduras, but to the eastern slopes of the Andes Mountains in the upper Amazon basin in what is modern-day Peru. However, we don't have the same archaeological evidence of its existence in the Amazon in pre-Hispanic times.

Additionally, there is no evidence that chocolate in any form was consumed in the upper Amazon basin. The indigenous tribes that have survived and still thrive in the Amazon to this day have no relationship to cacao other than to suck the sweet pulp of the cacao fruit off the seeds. What we have to go on instead is extensive genetic research that suggests that cacao slowly made its way from the Amazon to Mesoamerica over thousands of years by the slow travel of tribes down the Amazon and into Brazil, or up into Ecuador, and then up into Venezuela and Colombia before making its way to Central America. This may have happened by land, but more likely it was via a coastal trading route that would have likely stretched from northern Ecuador to Chiapas, Mexico. So it is that in Mesoamerica the history of chocolate begins.

Clay vessels from the Pacific coast of Chiapas in southern Mexico have been tested and found to contain both theobromine and caffeine, a combination of alkaloids that is unique to cacao in ancient Central America. These clay vessels are thought to have been from the Barra people, who far predate the Maya and the Aztecs. Carbon dating places these vessels at 1800 BCE, thus making it the earliest evidence of the use of chocolate on the planet. Nothing is known about the purpose of drinking chocolate by the Barras, and no Barra language exists for us to study.

Centuries later, on the Atlantic coast along the Mexican gulf, the first evidence of chocolate in language exists. The Olmec people, rulers of the Americas' first city, San Lorenzo, had a word for chocolate: *kakawa*. This word is said to have been used as far back as 1000 BCE Additionally, a bowl containing *kakawa* was found just outside the city of San Lorenzo, and has been dated to around 1350 BCE This would have also been the first word referencing cacao that the Spanish encountered in Yucatán from the Maya there, since it was a word the Maya adopted from the Olmec. *Kakaw* is the word for the social and ceremonial beverage that the Mayans prepared from cacao. The first evidence of chocolate in the area ruled by the Maya was found in a bowl at a temple site in northern Belize and dated 400 BCE. The Maya, who didn't begin to thrive as a civilization until the beginning of the Common Era, likely got their ceremonial and sanctified relationship with

cacao from the Izapan, a post-Olmec culture that ruled much of the land throughout Chiapas, the Yucatán, and northern Guatemala and Belize before the Maya.

We know the Maya held cacao in high regard. Many early Mayan hieroglyphic codices depict gods seated with cacao pods or with baskets of cacao seeds. Many also list specific quantities of cacao that should be sacramentally offered up to certain gods. One of the most important Mayan gods, the god of maize (corn), Ixim-te, is often depicted with a cacao tree growing out of his head. Mayan nobility were often buried with pots and dishes, often containing cacao drink or a cacao and maize porridge for sustenance in the afterlife. The Maya had many ornate pots for the preparation and storage of cacao. These pots often had recipes or lists of ingredients for specific chocolate drinks. From as early as 500 CE, there is evidence that Maya were putting chile peppers in their chocolate drink.

Around the same time, there is evidence that shows how to prepare a chocolate drink. A chocolate drink was to be prepared by transferring the beverage back and forth between two pots. One was to stand and pour the beverage from one pot into a pot on the ground. Pouring the beverage back and forth from this height caused the chocolate to create a foam. The creation of this foam became a ritual for weddings, funerals, coronations, feasts, sacrifices, and other special events.

There were certainly not just one or two standard recipes for a cacao-based beverage, but likely dozens of recipes for beverages served at different temperatures and with the inclusion of different fruits, flowers, spices, and chiles. A porridge containing cornmeal, cacao, and hot water was common, and much less ceremonial than other cacao recipes, and today this is still consumed by Mayan farmers in Guatemala. This porridge provides farmers with cheap sustenance to start their day and the cacao gives them a boost of energy as they head out into the fields. As the Mayan empire began to meet its downfall in the twelfth century, their conquerors, the Toltecs, would fight the Maya for control of the most fertile cacao-growing lands: Chontalpa in Tabasco, and the Pacific coast bordering the Chiapas and Guatemala.

HISTORY OF CHOCOLATE: SPANISH CONQUEST

The first record of chocolate discovery by the Europeans comes from an account by none other than Christopher Columbus during his fourth voyage to the New World in 1502. Columbus had set sail for the island of Jamaica after being forbidden from landing in Hispaniola, but missed wildly and ended up on the tiny island of Guanaja off the coast of Honduras. Here, he ordered the capture of some merchants who were traveling in a long palm wood canoe. These Mayan merchants were likely en route to Honduras from the southern tip of the Yucatán when they were intercepted by Columbus. Columbus was impressed by many of their wares, which included axes, Aztec-style weapons, maize beer, and cotton garments, but what caught his attention most were their strange "almonds" that they seemed to value higher than their other impressive wares, almost as if they were currency. These "almonds" were almost certainly cacao seeds. Columbus's brief encounter with the material that would later be used to make chocolate all over Europe shows just how prevalent it was in Mesoamerica at the time. Columbus would never find out just how important these almonds were to the indigenous peoples of the Americas, and he would never experience a chocolate drink, but even he knew in this brief encounter in 1502 what we know now, that chocolate and cacao were special.

The first Spanish account of how truly valued cacao and chocolate drink were comes from a soldier in Cortés's army by the name of Bernal Diaz del Castillo. He would have encountered the lavishness of chocolate in the Aztec empire sometime late in 1519 or early in 1520 at a meal Cortés and his men attended at the palace of Montezuma II. At this meal, Diaz recounts how more than 200 local dishes were served, but that instead of eating, Montezuma preferred to sit back and sip on a frothy drink made from cacao served in a gourd. Montezuma, in addition to serving this drink to his guests, ordered that the performers, cooks, and bakers be served the chocolate drink. When the meal was finished, 2,000 pots of chocolate were prepared to mark the conclusion of the festivities.

By the mid-sixteenth century, the Spanish conquistadors were beginning to drink chocolate themselves, but unlike the people of the Aztec empire, they preferred ingredients that weren't native to the Americas to mix with cacao. The chocolate beverages of the Aztecs were commonly served cold or at room temperature and were often unsweetened or sweetened with a hint of honey. These beverages were also enhanced by local flowers or spices like annatto, or even mixed with chile peppers, often for medicinal purposes. The Spanish found the ingredients and flavor of these beverages to be very strange, so they began to make a sweetened version of the drink with cane sugar. They also would flavor their version of the beverage with cinnamon, allspice, vanilla, or black pepper, which were all exotic spices they had been exposed to by previous conquests in the East. In the late sixteenth century, when dairy cows were brought over to the Americas, some Spaniards decided that they preferred chocolate beverages prepared with warm milk instead of water. In addition, Aztec warriors would carry small cakes or tablets of ground cacao with them into battle so that they could drink chocolate for strength at any time. The discovery of these tablets by the Spanish would eventually make the export of chocolate for drinking much easier.

When chocolate was first exported to Spain, at the turn of the seventeenth century, it was brought in mostly by wealthy, retired Spanish merchants. They would import it out of curiosity and to have something new to show off at parties. When it was first exported, not only did you need a lot of money to buy cacao and chocolate, but since news of new discoveries traveled slowly, you also had to be connected to the military or merchant community in some way to even know of its existence. Despite being experienced by Cortés and others in the first half of the sixteenth century, chocolate wasn't really experienced outside of the merchant elite in Spain until the second half of the seventeenth century. By that time, news of chocolate beverages had also made its way to Italy by way of the Catholic Church and their ever-expanding network of Papal States.

CHOCOLATE SWEEPS ACROSS EUROPE

Chocolate entered Europe in the age of alchemy and humorism, and as such, the humors of chocolate were analyzed by many an alchemist as the Old World tried to make sense of the medicinal properties of chocolate. Chocolate confounded much of the medical community at the time of its arrival. Let's quickly play out how a debate between three physicians of the Baroque period may have gone:

PHYSICIAN 1: Chocolate is clearly cold and moist. This is how the natives of the New World treat it in their preparation. Chocolate is clearly phlegmatic because those who imbibe too much of it become lazy and apathetic.

PHYSICIAN 2: While it is indeed served cold, chocolate also contains spices that heat it up. Some of the spices that the natives use even turn the beverage a blood-red color. I surmise that the qualities of these substances are warm and moist.

PHYSICIAN 3: I don't mean to be rude, but you are both incorrect on this matter. Let us not forget that chocolate is derived from cacao, and that cacao is both dry and cold. It is also important to note that the color of the cacao seed is black and that this is a substance forged by the earth. I surmise that phlegmatic behavior you deduce from its misuse is in fact misdiagnosed melancholy.

The humorist properties of chocolate would be debated throughout the Baroque period, through the Renaissance and into the age of enlightenment, but the general consensus appears to be that chocolate was prescribed to restore warmth to the body and to encourage blood flow, and because of such, was generally prescribed with warm spices like vanilla, cinnamon, and black pepper. It appears that many were warned that the overuse of chocolate would result in the body overheating or burning up. It was the Italians who got creative with their preparation of chocolate to encourage a balance of the humors so it could be consumed more regularly. Members of the court of Tuscany in the middle of the seventeenth century would add orange, lemon, jasmine flowers, and other perfumes to "cool" the traditionally "warm" beverage prepared all over Spain.

Altering the humors of chocolate wouldn't be the only creative thing the Italians would do when chocolate arrived in Italy. It was likely Italian chefs who first experimented with chocolate in food. Recipes started to appear in northern Italy in the late seventeenth century that included chocolate in sauces and meat dishes. There are even recipes for a chocolate lasagna that contained a sauce made from anchovies and chocolate. By the eighteenth century, the Italians had made cakes, mousses, puddings, and polentas that all contained chocolate.

Meanwhile in France, the perfection of the frothing and storage of the chocolate beverage was well under way. The Spanish had developed the *molinillo*, a bulbous wooden rod with rings on it that helped to aerate the chocolate and create foam, but the French found a way to embed it into the lid of a metal pot for making the chocolate drink, the *chocolatière*. This new method kept the chocolate from splashing or frothing out of your vessel while it was being prepared. Chocolate came into France from Spanish monks via the Cardinal of Lyon. In 1659, the first license for making and selling chocolate throughout France was granted to David Chaliou, a well-traveled chocolate lover, who had encountered the stuff in Spain.

The court of Louis the XIV served chocolate quite regularly for the better part of the back half of the seventeenth century. However, in 1693 he outlawed it from the palace, citing reasons of economy. In addition to the *chocolatière*, the French also diversified the way in which chocolate was manufactured for sale. In addition to the disks that were common throughout Spain, *pastilles* as the French called them, they also began selling chocolate by the box or brick, and in small daily serving-size pouches of chocolate liquor.

While the French and Italians were busy experimenting and innovating in the realm of this New World delicacy, the British were using chocolate the way the Aztecs did—lavishly. In the late seventeenth century, tea and coffee houses were popping up all over London. These became places of politics, art, science, and philosophy, as well as community centers and employment offices. The heartbeat of any London neighborhood was its tea or coffee house. It was natural then that when chocolate made its way to London that it would also get its own "house." The chocolate house in London turned out to be something different entirely from the scholarly and commerce driven tea or coffee house. A London chocolate house was a gentlemen's club where one could come to indulge in exotic and lavish chocolate drinks while gambling. The stories of the gambling that took place in the chocolate houses of London are scandalous, like the tale that at a house by the name of the Cocoa-Tree, 180,000 pounds was exchanged in one night of gambling. Or the disturbing story that came out of the notorious White's Chocolate House, that on one evening in 1750, a man collapsed on the steps of the club only to have the members begin to take bets on whether they thought the man was dead.

Though it had taken many forms and uses, by the middle of the eighteenth century, chocolate had swept through Europe.

Dutching in the Twenty-First Century

Dutching is still employed in the chocolate industry today by large companies, but for somewhat different reasons than in 1828. Turn over a mass-produced chocolate bar in the grocery store and you might find the phrase "cocoa produced with alkali." This process is done to remove bitterness and astringency from the flavor of the cocoa by washing it in sodium carbonates. If the original cocoa beans used are fermented and dried properly, the bitterness or astringency in the beans should show itself as mild acidity and fruity notes. Essentially, Dutch processing is used to strip poor-quality cocoa beans of their unique flavor compounds by making the pH of that cocoa neutral. This process also dramatically lowers the natural antioxidants found in cocoa. Good-quality natural cocoa powder contains a much more interesting and delicate flavor than the dark, bland, neutral flavor of the Dutch-processed cocoa that is found in most cookies, ice creams, cakes, and many chocolate bars. (See page 46.)

THE WORLD'S FIRST CHOCOLATE FACTORIES

By the eighteenth century, chocolate factories were not uncommon throughout Europe. These were small shops designed specifically to refine cacao for use in making chocolate drink. What is peculiar about these early chocolate factories is how virtually no innovations were made in the processing of chocolate from the time of the Olmecs all the way to the dawn of the industrial period. If you were to walk into a chocolate factory in Spain or France in 1780, you would find the same technique of making chocolate that was employed by the Aztecs, and the Maya before them, and on down the lineage in the history of making chocolate. In the late eighteenth century, cacao was still roasted by hand and ground by hand using a stone metate. The first mechanized chocolate equipment appears to have not been from Europe at all, but from a factory in the English colony of Massachusetts. John Hannon and James Baker used a gristmill at Lower Milton Falls in Dorchester in 1765 to grind cocoa beans using water power. The Baker Chocolate Company, as it later became known, would continue to make chocolate in Massachusetts for 200 years, until it was moved to Delaware in 1965.

The biggest breakthrough, however, in the mass commercialization of chocolate would come from a Dutchman in 1828. In the nineteenth century, people had begun to theorize that removing the fat from the cocoa nibs would make chocolate more easily digestible. It was chemist and chocolate maker Coenraad Johannes van Houten who would be the one to crack this cocoa bean wide open in his factory in Holland. Van Houten invented a hydraulic press that reduced the cocoa butter content of the cocoa nibs by half. The result of removing half the fat from the cocoa nibs was a cake of pure cocoa. This cake could be easily ground up into a powder. Cocoa powder would make chocolate accessible to many more people. No longer did you need a fancy *chocolatière* to produce chocolate drink: You could simply stir cocoa powder into hot water. To improve cocoa's miscibility, van Houten also invented Dutching, a process of treating cocoa with alkalized

salts. This process also darkens cocoa powder and mellows its natural acidity.

The Fry family had been churning out chocolate products in England since 1728. By the mid-nineteenth century, the Frys had established themselves as England's first family of chocolate, a third-generation powerhouse that was about to change the face of chocolate forever. In 1847, under the supervision of the founder's grandson, Francis Fry, the company found a way to make a less viscous chocolate paste by recombining cocoa powder with melted cocoa butter and sugar. This mixture could be easily poured into molds and was smooth and pleasant compared to the brittle French chocolate "boxes." At an exhibition in Birmingham in 1849, Francis Fry and his son, Joseph Storrs Fry, introduced the world for the first time to the chocolate bar. This bar was not meant to be melted down in water, but was instead meant to be taken by itself in a solid form. As a result of this discovery, cocoa butter prices went through the roof, and once again the most desirable form of chocolate would remain an indulgence of the elite.

At the end of the century, Swiss chemist Henri Nestlé discovered a way to powderize dairy milk. This discovery would prompt Milton Hershey to replace most of the cocoa butter in chocolate bars with milk fat to lower the cost of the product, hence making it accessible to a much larger audience.

THE DARK SIDE OF CHOCOLATE

The history of chocolate may seem like mostly fun and games, but it's important to remember that a lot of bloodshed had to take place for us to enjoy the product that we all hold so dear now. The origin of chocolate comes from the Spanish empire's merciless slaughter of the Aztec people on the Mexican plains. We also know that the Aztec were no angels themselves, enslaving or sacrificing anyone in their path. Because no cacao grows in the high plains of Tenochtitlan, modern-day Mexico City, the royals of Montezuma's court made the people of the lowlands bring them their most-prized crop as a bribe to keep Aztec armies from slaughtering them.

When you examine the early days of cacao plantations in Ecuador and Venezuela and across the Caribbean, cacao was almost always produced for export to the Old World by slaves. These slaves were brought from West Africa on Dutch and Portuguese trading vessels and often traded to cacao plantation owners in exchange for cacao to bring back to Europe. When cacao was brought from Brazil to Africa by the Portuguese in the nineteenth century, it traveled there around the time slavery was outlawed by most European countries. This timing is hardly a coincidence. The end of the Atlantic slave trade marked a collapse in the economies of West Africa. This caused the farming of cacao in West Africa to become very affordable as the demand for chocolate bars went up.

To this day, the lack of strong labor laws in West Africa, particularly Ghana and the Ivory Coast, make producing cacao with low-cost labor appealing to world's largest chocolate-producing corporations. Such lack of labor laws often leads to human rights violations and always leads to extreme poverty. In 2016, the World Bank listed the global poverty line at $2 per person per day. In that same year, according to Cocoa Barometer, a group tasked by international NGOs to study and report on ways to improve poverty in cacao farming, the average income for a cocoa farmer in Ivory Coast and Ghana was less than $0.70 per person per day. The Ivory Coast and Ghana combined produce half of the world's cocoa supply. Annually, cacao production represents 40 to 50 percent of the total export economies of both these countries. The average life expectancy in the United States, France, and Spain is 81.5 years. In the Ivory Coast and Ghana, it is 57.8 years. Slavery has been abolished in most of the far reaches of the globe, but it is important to remember that exploitation still exists and that consumption sometimes comes at a grave cost. Chocolate is certainly not immune.

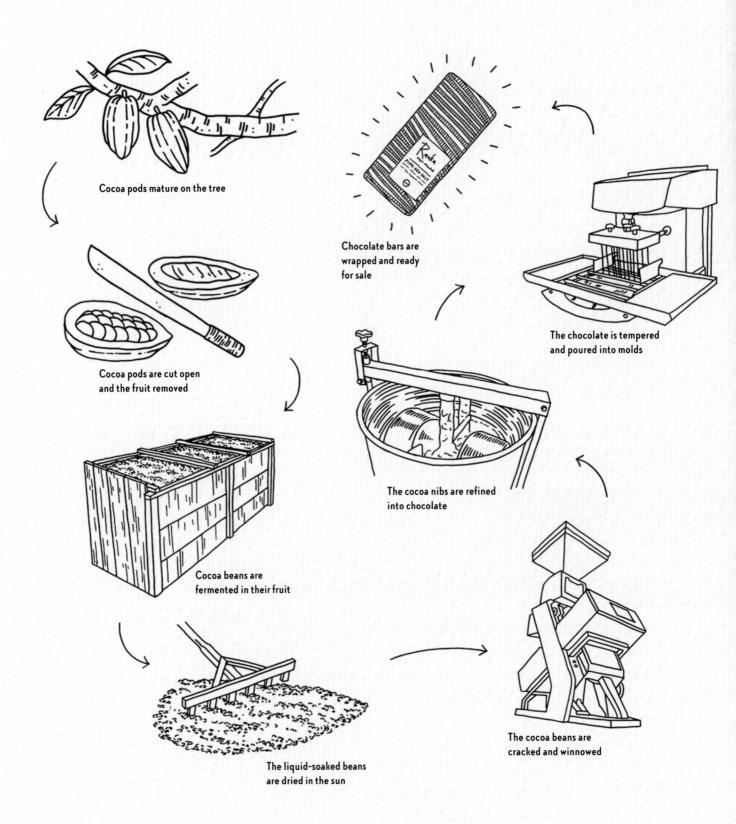

Cocoa pods mature on the tree

Cocoa pods are cut open and the fruit removed

Cocoa beans are fermented in their fruit

The liquid-soaked beans are dried in the sun

The cocoa beans are cracked and winnowed

The cocoa nibs are refined into chocolate

The chocolate is tempered and poured into molds

Chocolate bars are wrapped and ready for sale

CHAPTER 2

BEAN-TO-BAR CHOCOLATE

The history of chocolate may be checkered, but the future doesn't have to be. This attitude is what is at the core of Raaka. We believe we have a commitment to educate people on the past wrongdoings in the chocolate industry, but also to communicate and collaborate on ways to move forward in a more equitable manner. Do a quick Internet search and find where the closest small bean-to-bar factory is to your house. Take a trip to it and ask to speak with the owners or a manager; I assure you, they'll be happy to talk to you about this very commitment, or something like it. Education, exceptional quality, and social equity are the pillars that bean-to-bar chocolate stands on. So how does bean-to-bar chocolate differ from other chocolate, or mass-produced chocolate, and what does the phrase even mean?

DEFINING BEAN-TO-BAR CHOCOLATE

Bean-to-bar chocolate begins when the same person or company that is purchasing cocoa beans is the same person or company that is actively taking those beans through all the steps of the chocolate-making process to a finished product ready for retail. This is a different process than how most of the world's chocolate is produced. Most of the world's chocolate is made in a handful of very large chocolate factories, mostly in Europe. These factories produce either chocolate liquor or chocolate couverture (bulk chocolate). This bulk chocolate product is then sent to another factory for mixing with sugar, milk powder, additional cocoa butter, Dutch-processed cocoa powder, and other flavorings. The chocolate is then molded into whatever bar or candy the factory produces. You've seen and probably eaten this kind of chocolate often, from a convenient store or supermarket. It usually doesn't mention the percentage of cocoa in the product, and almost never lists the country the chocolate or the cocoa nibs came from. Bean-to-bar chocolate is a response to this nameless, untraceable (to the consumer) bulk chocolate product that exists all over the globe.

EXCEPTIONAL QUALITY

At Raaka we believe that bean-to-bar chocolate should start first and foremost with a chocolate that is of exceptional quality. The quality of the product informs everything else we do. This is an attitude that is shared throughout the bean-to-bar chocolate world. The raw materials that we start with need to be the best available for us to produce high-quality chocolate. From our cane sugar and sweeteners to the cocoa butter we use and the whole ingredients we add to our chocolate, we choose all of them deliberately, with their quality being the main driver. This is especially true of our cocoa beans, which we choose through relationships we forge in the countries where they are grown. For Raaka, the fermentation and drying of our cocoa beans are as important as the process we put those beans through when they reach our factory.

As the saying goes, "You can put lipstick on a pig, but it is still a pig." When it comes to chocolate, you can process your cocoa with alkali, pump it full of milk fat and sugar, but you're likely doing that to hide the unpleasantness of the flavors of the cocoa beans you've started with. Bean-to-bar chocolate is a proclamation of the quality of the cocoa beans that are being used, as if to say, "Look at these cocoa beans I bought from my friends Simran and Brian from the Kilombero Valley of central Tanzania—don't they have a unique flavor? Here, compare them to the beans I bought from my friends Charles and Ramón from the hills of the north coast of the Dominican Republic. Aren't the two wildly different?" It's that level of traceability and pride in the quality raw materials that makes bean-to-bar chocolate special, and different from mass-produced chocolate.

COMMITMENT TO SOCIAL EQUITY

Cocoa farming is one of the poorest professions on the planet. There are a number of third-party certifications like Fair Trade, Rainforest Alliance, and Fair-for-Life that seek to protect cocoa farmers against extremely low wages. These programs do a good job of raising the floor for what cacao farmers can make, but they don't necessarily protect them against the perils of commodity trading. The commodity market dictates the cost of cocoa beans, and it fluctuates dramatically. In November 2015, cocoa prices reached a ten-year high of $3,360 per metric ton (1,000 kg), but in April 2017, they reached a six-year low of $1,961. These prices are not what the farmers make, but rather what the export price is. Farmers whose cacao is sold on the commodity market are making anywhere from 40 to 50 percent less than what cacao is being traded at per kilogram. That means that in April 2017, they were making slightly over $1 per kilogram, while back in November 2015, they were making around $1.70 per kilogram. The certifications that exist to protect cacao farmers typically pay a premium on top of whatever the commodity market is, so these farmers' incomes can still drastically shift from one year to the next. This makes it hard for farmers to budget the money they need for supplies to run their farm from year to year.

The goal of Raaka and other like-minded chocolate companies is to work with farmers long-term to raise the quality of cocoa beans that are being exported from a given farm, cooperative, or region. In doing so, the hope is to create a stable market that is not dictated by the perils of commodity trading but is built on quality, trust, and a communication of needs. Whereas the commodity market fluctuates, the bean-to-bar market seeks to create stability through relationships.

Let me give you an example of how this works. Gualberto and Adriano run Oko Caribe in the Dominican Republic, a small (by Dominican standards) cocoa bean–processing facility and export company. I have been buying cocoa beans directly from them for four years. We agreed that we would negotiate our price every year in person. So each year I visit Gualberto and Adriano, we tour the facility, they take me out to their favorite local lunch spot, and then we negotiate a price on the cocoa beans for that year. Oftentimes, I will also negotiate on behalf of other chocolate companies that trust me and

Raaka so that we can consolidate shipment. Gualberto and Adriano pay above the Dominican market rate to their farmers to promote quality and loyalty. They also provide training programs on farm and soil management to help the farmers that work with them manage both their finances and their land so that they can maximize both. Every year I meet with them, I learn something new about their commitment to their community, and we agree on a price that is fair and consistent with previous years. Here are the prices Raaka has paid (per metric ton) Gualberto and Adriano for cocoa beans and what they've paid to their farmers:

2014: $3,900 to Oko Caribe, $2,600 to the farmers
2015: $4,100 to Oko Caribe, $2,700 to the farmers
2016: $4,100 to Oko Caribe, $2,900 to the farmers
2017: $4,000 to Oko Caribe, $2,700 to the farmers

Again, if you find your local bean-to-bar chocolate maker and ask about the quality of their cocoa beans and their commitment to social equity, they'll all approach it somewhat differently but with the same principles in mind. They may collaborate with other chocolate companies, or purchase through a third-party that has sustainability and traceability commitments, but the ethos is all generally aligned.

PART II

RECIPES AND TECHNIQUES

CHAPTER 3

THE CHOCOLATE-MAKING PROCESS

As with many things, you can learn a lot about something and still feel like you know nothing: Welcome to chocolate. Scratching the surface of the origins and history of chocolate is a first peek into the process of making chocolate. In this chapter, I'll teach you the basics of chocolate making in the hope that you will learn to make rudimentary chocolate at home. I'm a strong believer in experimentation, and I hope the basic techniques you'll learn will provoke you to experiment with creative new techniques in your kitchen. Chocolate starts as a bean that is transported through a series of labor-intensive stages over many days until it becomes chocolate. It's a messy journey, so heed the warning, and designate some clothing as chocolate-making clothing in the same way you would designate clothes for painting. Okay, now let's get messy.

CHOOSING A COCOA BEAN

Everyone who works to craft anything must carefully choose the raw materials with which they will work. A potter must choose the right clay. A woodworker must choose the right type of wood. A winemaker must choose the right grapes. As the rule goes, a chocolate maker must choose the right cocoa bean. As we discussed in previous chapters, many factors play a role in the flavor of a cocoa bean, from genetics to terroir to fermentation and drying quality and techniques. These are things that, when starting out, can be difficult for beginning chocolate makers to even get information on.

Grading cocoa beans is complicated, but there are few tricks of the trade that will help when determining the quality of the beans you're about to work with.

Look at the exterior color of the beans. An even color with little variation is a good sign. It's an even better sign if the beans are brown with a slight hue of red. These beans were likely fermented, dried, and stored properly. Really dark brown or black beans are a sign of over-fermentation or even rot. Beans that have a shade of powdery white likely have developed exterior mold. This doesn't necessarily mean

there's anything wrong with the nibs themselves or the fermentation of the beans. This likely means that there was a problem with humidity and moisture during storage, which can signify other problems, but not always. Differentiation in color can mean that many lots, with varying degrees of quality, were all blended together.

Weigh 3 ½ ounces (100 g) of cocoa beans and count how many cocoa beans there are. This will give you an idea of what your yield will be. The more cocoa beans there are, the more shell there is, and that's something to keep in mind when pricing your raw materials. If you have small beans, it may be worth extra money per batch if those beans taste phenomenal.

Take fifty cocoa beans and cut them down the thinner side of the bean so you can see their cross section. This is called a cut test. Examine the inside of these beans and note how many are purple. Write this number down. This is roughly how you determine the level of fermentation in your cocoa beans. If you have twenty-five brown beans and twenty-five purple beans, you have 50 percent fermentation, which is not good. Also look for signs of interior mold or signs of webbing from bug infestation. If you have both of these things, you're probably not dealing with very high-quality cocoa beans, and you may want to reevaluate your source. Also note the depth of the fissures, or grooves, in the beans. Really deep fissures combined with brittle beans are a sign of over-fermentation. The presence of pencil-width grooves and a lot of purple means the beans are under-fermented. Dark beans with pencil-width grooves likely means that the beans were fermented for too long and didn't reach the proper temperature during the early stages of fermentation. Ideally you'll have 80 to 95 percent fermented or brown beans with deep fissures. If you have this, then you've likely found some pretty good beans. If you don't, you may have found some beans with interesting flavors, but be warned that it also likely means that beans from this source will be inconsistent, and the flavors you've found that you like in these beans might not be there in subsequent purchases.

ROASTING

Cocoa beans are roasted to promote the flavors that develop through the Maillard reaction. This reaction occurs between sugars and amino acids during a cooking process to unlock the flavors of things that can properly turn brown through cooking. It's the reason why seared meat always tastes better than boiled meat and why caramel has a complex and different flavor from table sugar. In the case of chocolate, roasting the cocoa beans is what gives chocolate its fudginess, so to speak. Many craft chocolate makers around the globe are opting for an extremely light roast over the times and temperatures traditionally associated with chocolate, encouraging less of a Maillard reaction in exchange for flavors developed during fermentation. When cocoa beans are properly fermented, they can possess flavors as complex as ripe pitted fruits, fresh citrus peel, or even newly cut spring herbs and flowers. Many chocolate makers, yours truly especially, would rather opt for preserving these complex flavors than opt for chocolate that tastes, for lack of a better word, commercial. As a result, the range of flavors that people associate with chocolate is expanding and the perception of what chocolate is and can be is changing.

Roasting in an Oven: Convection Roasting

Preheat your oven to 250°F (120°C, or gas mark ½). On a baking sheet (preferably perforated), arrange cocoa beans in a single layer.

Put the beans on the middle rack of the oven. After about 7 minutes, open the oven door and use a wooden spoon or spatula to stir and turn over the beans.

After another few minutes, you'll start to smell that Maillard reaction, which will smell almost like brownies. Roast the beans for an additional 7 to 10 minutes, until you're pleased with the smell in your kitchen.

When you remove the beans from the oven, quickly transfer them to a cool baking sheet so they stop cooking. Play with times and temps that you like personally when it comes to roasting cocoa in your oven, but keep in mind 200°F to 325°F (93°C to 165°C) is the range that cocoa beans like best.

Drum Roasting

The best way to simulate basic drum roasting at home is by using a popcorn air popper. It doesn't stir cocoa beans as well as a real drum roaster does, but the basic principles of balanced convective and conductive apply in the mechanics of its design.

You will not have control over temperature the same way you do with a drum roaster or an oven, but you will have control over the time and the use of your senses to determine when your beans are roasted.

Place enough cocoa beans in the popper barrel so that it's about three-quarters full. Turn on the popper and stand by. After 3 minutes, you should be able to begin to smell the "browning" aroma. Let the popper run for about 6 minutes, and then remove one of your cocoa beans and taste it. You should receive a pretty good roast in only a few minutes. You'll only be able to roast a few beans at a time using an air-popper, but it is a good simulation.

Small home coffee roasters are available online for under $350. If you're serious about drum-roasting cocoa, picking up one of these may prove essential.

At the end of the day, however, it all comes down to personal preference, and if you like chocolate that has more fudgy, malty-like flavors, then hotter roasting may be for you. As we'll find with most equipment for chocolate, you have options when choosing your method for roasting.

Different cocoa beans will have different variables to consider when roasting. Things like the size of the bean, the thickness of the shell, the moisture level of the bean, and the relative fat content of the nib will have huge effects on how you roast. Because of this, chocolate makers must consider time, temperature, and roasting method for each type of cocoa bean they work with. A chocolate maker may choose to do dozens of different test roasts for each new bean they receive, to determine the ideal roast.

ROASTING IN A CONVECTION OVEN

This method of roasting uses hot air to heat the environment around your cocoa beans, causing them to bake, or roast, in the same way you would bake bread or a cake in your own oven.

Convection oven roasting can be tricky because different pockets of the oven can have different temperatures. Also, the direct heat or conductive heat of perforated sheet trays and oven racks can prove inconsistent. These things can result in an uneven roast, so the oven tends to be best for shorter, hotter roasts.

The art of convection oven roasting is about being attuned to sights, sounds, and smells in addition to dialing in the correct time and temperature. This method of roasting cocoa beans is the easiest to get started with, since you probably own an oven.

DRUM ROASTING

A drum roaster is a type of roaster that is used for both coffee and cocoa beans. The main goal of a drum roaster is to use both convective and conductive heating in a way that is even and consistent throughout the roaster. A drum roaster operates with a perforated barrel-shaped drum placed on its side over a series of burners. The burners heat both the air around the drum and the drum itself. The drum rotates on a single axis so that the metal of the drum is heated evenly. As it turns, it mixes the beans that are placed in it so that, ideally, each bean comes in contact with the same amount of hot air as it does hot metal. When the roast is done, the beans can be released into a secondary, cool, open-air drum that cools the beans evenly.

This type of roasting is the preferred method for chocolate makers because of the amount of control you can have. The emphasis on even roasting also allows you to roast at lower temperatures for longer periods of time with relative ease. Software programs now exist that allow you to monitor and data-log the temperature fluctuation that occurs within a drum roaster. This level of control helps with consistency and with learning the science behind how times and temperatures affect the flavor development of your cocoa beans.

CRACKING AND WINNOWING COCOA BEANS

The first challenge of the chocolate-making process is getting the pesky shell on the outside of the bean to break off. Depending on how much moisture loss you achieve in your roast, this can be a challenge for a chocolate maker of any skill level. Like the nibs, the shells contain theobromine, but unlike the nibs, they don't contain very much fat and are instead full of fiber. Fiber is sort of the unspoken enemy of chocolate. It impedes the natural fat of the cocoa nibs and the smoothness of chocolate. It's important to remove all of the shell when making chocolate to avoid any imperfect textures in the finished product. The first step in this process is breaking, or cracking, the beans.

CRACKING COCOA BEANS

To break a cocoa bean, all you really need is intense force and moderate to severe pressure. In a chocolate factory, this can be achieved with a number of different types of machines. A large burr grinder like one that is used to grind coffee can be used

to crack cocoa beans. The beans can also be fed through a set of studded rollers, forcing the shells to burst off the nibs. Cocoa beans can be dropped into a chamber with spinning metal arms or blades, to be broken on impact. Once the beans are cracked, a mixture of nibs and shells remain. These need to be separated through a process called winnowing.

WINNOWING COCOA BEANS

The term *winnow* is one that refers back to the production of wheat. To separate the wheat grains from the chaff, one must toss the cracked wheat in the air and allow the wind to carry away the chaff. This is exactly how it is traditionally done in the production of chocolate in Mesoamerican cultures. A bowl of nibs and shell are tossed into the air repeatedly until the wind has blown all the shell away. Inside a chocolate factory, there isn't a whole lot of wind, so this natural process must be simulated with a machine aptly called a winnower.

Different methods of simulation are used, leveraging the same physical properties as natural winnowing. On a commercial scale, a large density-based sorter is common. Because the nibs weigh a lot more than the shell, they can be sorted with different sizes of screens and vibration. With this type of machine, you collect different sizes of nibs and shells out of various screens and shoot them into buckets. The way this machine shakes and dumps material out of various chutes makes it look like the kind of whimsical, wacky machine usually associated with fictional chocolate factories.

The easiest way to winnow on a relatively small commercial scale is using gravity and suction as the mechanisms for sorting. The nibs fall faster than the shells, so if you apply a bit of suction via a vacuum or other device as they fall, you can remove the shells without changing the general trajectory of the nibs. People have optimized these general physics with commercial equipment and homemade contraptions alike. The first winnower I used was built by a friend out of 2x4s, PVC, and a wet-dry vacuum; now I use a robot.

An optical sorter can also be used to separate nibs and shell. It is a machine that uses artificial intelligence to identify "bad material"—in this case, cocoa shells. The machined is programmed with photos of the materials that will be run through the machine. The good material is photographed and highlighted, as is the bad material. When the mixture of materials runs through the main shaft of the machine, the machine scans it and rejects the bad material, or in this case cocoa shells, with the sixty small airstreams it controls. This type of

machine is also used for sorting grains of rice and for removing burnt pieces of cereal in a cereal factory. One day, when it gains enough intelligence, it may even run my factory for me. I'd clarify that I'm joking, but I'm afraid it might hear me and I'm hoping it treats me well in the future when I work for it.

WASTE IN COCOA BEANS

When a winnow is successful, the ratio of nib to shell should be about 4 to 1. That's a lot of shells for a chocolate factory to produce in a year. My factory produces 10,000 to 12,000 pounds (4,536 to 5,443 kg) of cocoa shells on an annual basis, and we're extremely small. Roughly 11 million pounds (4.9 million kg) of cacao is produced globally on an annual basis, which means about 2 million pounds (more than 907,000 kg) of cocoa shells are generated. Though these cannot be used for chocolate production, they do have a variety of other useful applications.

Roasted cocoa shells are often used in teas to add chocolaty flavor. Since they contain theobromine, they taste similar to nibs when you steep nibs, but they are cheaper and don't add as much unwanted fatty oil to a tea as nibs. They're often blended with teas, or can be steeped and drunk on their own.

Cocoa shells are also fantastic for gardening. Because they are high in nitrogen, they break down quickly and when put with other vegetal refuse can cause other materials to decompose quicker, making a rich and nutrient-filled addition to soil. They're often used as a brown material in compost or placed directly in a garden as a kind of mulch/natural fertilizer. At Raaka, we give all our shells to rooftop farms and after-school gardening programs. It has helped us form some great relationships with people doing very interesting and important work in urban areas.

GRINDING COCOA NIBS

The act of grinding cocoa nibs is what turns the crunchy raw material into a smooth, shiny, flowing substance that resembles liquid chocolate. Cocoa nibs are made up of roughly 50 percent cocoa butter, a fat, and 50 percent cocoa powder, a solid. The first step in making cocoa nibs into chocolate is to turn those nibs into cocoa liquor. When we grind cocoa nibs, our goal is to use friction and tension to accomplish two key things in the creation of chocolate.

The first thing we want to accomplish is the heating and release of the cocoa butter present in the cocoa nibs. This fat, when heated and released, is what will give the chocolate its flow, its ability to be easily moved from one machine to another in a liquid state.

The second thing we want to accomplish when we grind cocoa nibs is the refinement of the cocoa particles present in the solids of the cocoa powder. For this, we need tension of some kind to reduce the size of the cocoa powder particles. If this is all sounding far too scientific, I assure you it is not, or else I wouldn't be able to understand it. I like to think about it this way. Say you want to make bread crumbs from a loaf of bread. The first thing you'll have to do is slice the loaf of bread, and then cut those slices into cubes. You'll then likely want to toast those chunks of bread to remove their moisture and make them easy to break up into smaller pieces. After you've essentially made croutons, you'll want to put those croutons in a blender or food processor and pulse them into the size bread crumbs you want. There, now you've taken a solid (a loaf of bread) and greatly reduced its particle size into many smaller bread crumbs.

That's just how chocolate is made: We've taken cocoa beans, and through a series of steps broken them down into cocoa nibs (i.e. croutons) and now in our grinding step, through tension, we're refining the particles in our cocoa powder into many microscopic particles. However, this process is rarely as straightforward as making bread crumbs. There are theories and competing schools of thought about the best way to refine cocoa particles, and I while won't describe them all here, I will walk through the basic mechanics of the machines that can be used to accomplish this refinement.

Cracking cocoa beans at home is not as easy as it may seem, as the fat complicates things. Attempting to crack them in a food processor can create just enough friction to begin to release the fats in the cocoa and leave you with a sticky, shell-ridden mess. So you're going to have to do it manually.

Put 2 cups (240 g) cocoa beans on a hard surface and press down on them with a rolling pin to release the shells. You can also put your beans in a large mortar and pestle and crack them the same way you crack spices. The best way to crack cocoa beans at home is to use a home-brewing roller mill. They are relatively inexpensive and can also be used for home brewing if you've always wanted to take up beer making.

Home winnowing is a blast. You'll need a few household items that you might not expect: a large cardboard box, a hair dryer, and a large wooden bowl. Simply place the box on its side on a table facing you. Fill the wooden bowl about two-thirds full with your nib and shell mixture and place the bowl in the box. Turn on the hair dryer and point it at the bowl from about 2 feet (60 cm) away. You'll then see the shells start to fly out of the bowl. Continue to hold the hair dryer pointed at the bowl, but use your free hand to shake the bowl to pull more shells up to the surface of the bowl. Once they come to the surface, the air from the hair dryer should blow them away. When your nibs are clean, you should have collected most of your shells in the box. You can empty the box into a bag so that you can save your shells for gardening. Now you have nibs and mulch.

LIQUORING

This is the process of taking the nibs and turning them into a wet paste or rough liquid. Liquoring can be done in a number of ways. Commercial stand mixers, peanut grinders, and juicers can all be used on a small scale. On a larger scale, roll mills (which we'll discuss later), pin mills, hammer mills, and plate mills are all used to make cocoa liquor quickly. These machines all have different mechanisms but are essentially the same in their design. They all contain a fast-spinning blade or plate that forces the cocoa nibs to rub up against a tight space. The friction caused by this rubbing allows the cocoa butter in the nibs to release and the liquoring process to begin. This step can be optional in some factories, but it is preferred by many for the controls it allows for in the later steps of processing chocolate. It also speeds up the chocolate-making process quite a bit.

Hack It at Home: Liquoring

Liquoring at home is easy. Simply put 2 cups (240 g) cocoa nibs into a small food processor and blend away. After 30 seconds or so, you should start to see some liquor begin to form on the outside walls of your food processor. At this point, turn off the continuous feature and pulse the nibs. This is important, because once your dry nibs start to turn into a paste, you'll want to be careful that the viscosity does force your food processor to overheat or jam up.

Pulse on and off for about 2 minutes. Every 30 seconds, open the food processor and scrape down the sides with a spatula so that you're getting an even blend. Scrape the liquor out of the food processor and into a small ovenproof dish. You may want to hold the liquor in the oven at its lowest heat setting until you're ready to use it.

MÉLANGEUR

Mélangeur is a French word that translates as "mixer." This machine is the first of many Swiss contributions to the world of chocolate. It was designed in 1826 by Philippe Suchard, who decided to start his own chocolate factory at a young age after realizing that chocolate cost more than three days of good wages at the time. The basic design of this machine is two large stones resting on a stone base, with tension being applied from the top. The friction from the stone-on-stone action present in this machine is the heat needed to coax the fat out of the cocoa nibs. The tension applied, if tight enough, will reduce the particle size of the cocoa solids (or cocoa powder) to a size that's too small to be significantly felt on the human palate.

This machine can be used as a step in the process of commercial chocolate making, or it can serve for home use and in small bean-to-bar chocolate shops as the only machine needed to turn nibs into finished chocolate liquor. Also often referred to as a wet grinder, it can also be used for processing bean pastes, chili pastes, and masa (Mexican cornmeal) into a beautiful texture and as a result can be found in a variety of sizes online. This type of processing isn't without its drawbacks for chocolate, though.

A batch of chocolate can take up to 4 days to process and still contain flaws. It is also very difficult to control flavor development with this type of machine, as it is both refining and aerating the chocolate at the same time. Things like internal temperature of the machine and the ambient temperature and humidity of the room play a big role in the flavor of the chocolate that's made. If you're serious about getting into chocolate making at home, the easiest way to do it is by picking up a small wet grinder online for a few hundred dollars. It's a purchase you won't regret, and it will come in handy to complete several recipes found in this book.

BALL MILL

A ball mill is a loud and powerful machine. It's a large cylindrical-shaped mixer that is filled with steel ball bearings. The mixing arms of the machine smash the ball bearings against each other over and over again. The partially refined chocolate liquor that's put in the machine gets trapped between the bearings and refined to less than 20 microns in size. The chocolate must enter this machine in a semiliquid state, so a pre-refining step is a necessity. A ball mill is super-efficient, and can do the work of a *mélangeur* in roughly a fifth of the time, depending on what version of the machine is being used. The ball mill's main drawback is that it's still possible to get outlier particles that can give the chocolate a slightly gritty texture. Also, while there is a lot of control in this method of refinement, it only refines, so unlike some other machines, a secondary flavor development step is necessary for making the finished chocolate product.

Hack It at Home: Making Chocolate in a Ball Mill

It's easy to make a simple ball mill at home. And this simple home-hacked machine will allow you to make chocolate.

What you need:

A 5-quart (4.8 L) stand mixer

3 pounds (1.4 kg) food-grade, stainless steel ball bearings (¼ inch, or 6 mm)

2 to 3 tablespoons (27 to 41 g) cocoa butter

2 cups (475 ml) cocoa liquor

¾ cup (150 g) sugar

Attach the dough kneading attachment to the stand mixer. Fill the mixing bowl with 1 pound (455 g) of the ball bearings. Melt the cocoa butter in the microwave for 30 seconds. Pour the melted cocoa butter over the ball bearings to grease them up. Turn the mixer on for 5 seconds to "charge" the balls. Add the rest of the ball bearings, ½ pound (225 g) at a time, and repeat the charging step each time. Once you've charged all the balls, turn the mixer on medium speed and slowly pour the cocoa liquor into the mixer.

After about 10 minutes, slowly add the sugar. Allow the mixer to run for another 25 to 30 minutes, until your mixture is smooth. Monitor the temperature of your stand mixer to make sure it isn't overheating.

Pour the chocolate and the ball bearings over a strainer into a bowl to collect the chocolate.

THREE-ROLL AND FIVE-ROLL MILLS

Now here is our great equalizer. The roll mill is used to refine, but also to even out, the cocoa particle size distribution of the chocolate. The machine is three or five steel rolls spaced very close together, essentially touching. Think of a traditional pasta maker, with its rollers. The first two rolls of the mill roll toward each other and the chocolate is fed onto them. The second and third rolls roll away from each other as the chocolate is squeezed between the first two rolls and then squeezed again between rolls two and three and transferred from the third roll to some kind of offshoot. For a five-roll mill, you just repeat the first two steps again. Each space that the chocolate is pulled through is tightened in sequential order, with loosest roll in the back and the tightest roll in the front. Chocolate, not cocoa liquor, is usually passed through a roll mill in a semi-refined state. This means that the chocolate should be above 20 microns in particle size, because the goal in a roll mill is to refine all the particles to an even distribution just below that threshold. A roll mill is used as an intermediary step between a primary or secondary refinement step like a *mélangeur* or a ball mill and a conching step, which we'll talk about next. While a ball mill is efficient at reducing particle size, the tight space that the chocolate is pulled through causes the particles to get flattened. Great chocolate has particles that are rounded like pearls and roll down your tongue. The particles that come off a roll mill will stick into or onto your tongue, which is why additional processing is needed. Its precision is really what makes a roll mill appealing.

CONCHING CHOCOLATE

Once you've refined your chocolate, there's an important flavor development stage called conching. This process is done to massage both the flavor molecules and the cocoa particles while aerating the chocolate. Conching rounds your cocoa particles into beautiful microscopic pearls and evenly coats them in the fat of the cocoa butter so that you have a silky smooth, full mouthfeel. Conching is used to drive out acidity by making sure as many of the flavor compounds as possible are coming in contact with as much air as possible. This sounds more complex than it is; it's really just vigorous mixing with the addition of natural or forced air.

There are many different contraptions that can be used to conch. The best way to send a chocolate maker down a philosophical rabbit hole is to ask him or her about the importance of conching and the best method or machine for conching.

Different chocolate companies conch for vastly different periods of time. I've seen conching times vary from as short as 2 hours to as long as 72 hours. The unspoken agreed-upon middle is more common, something like 12 to 36 hours.

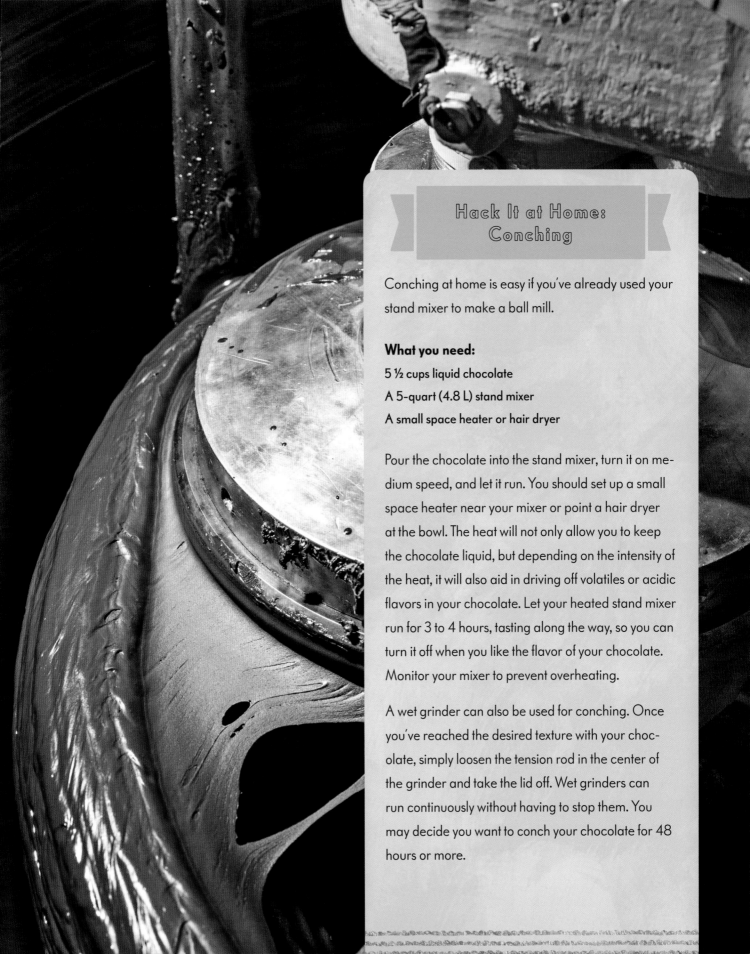

Hack It at Home: Conching

Conching at home is easy if you've already used your stand mixer to make a ball mill.

What you need:
5 ½ cups liquid chocolate
A 5-quart (4.8 L) stand mixer
A small space heater or hair dryer

Pour the chocolate into the stand mixer, turn it on medium speed, and let it run. You should set up a small space heater near your mixer or point a hair dryer at the bowl. The heat will not only allow you to keep the chocolate liquid, but depending on the intensity of the heat, it will also aid in driving off volatiles or acidic flavors in your chocolate. Let your heated stand mixer run for 3 to 4 hours, tasting along the way, so you can turn it off when you like the flavor of your chocolate. Monitor your mixer to prevent overheating.

A wet grinder can also be used for conching. Once you've reached the desired texture with your chocolate, simply loosen the tension rod in the center of the grinder and take the lid off. Wet grinders can run continuously without having to stop them. You may decide you want to conch your chocolate for 48 hours or more.

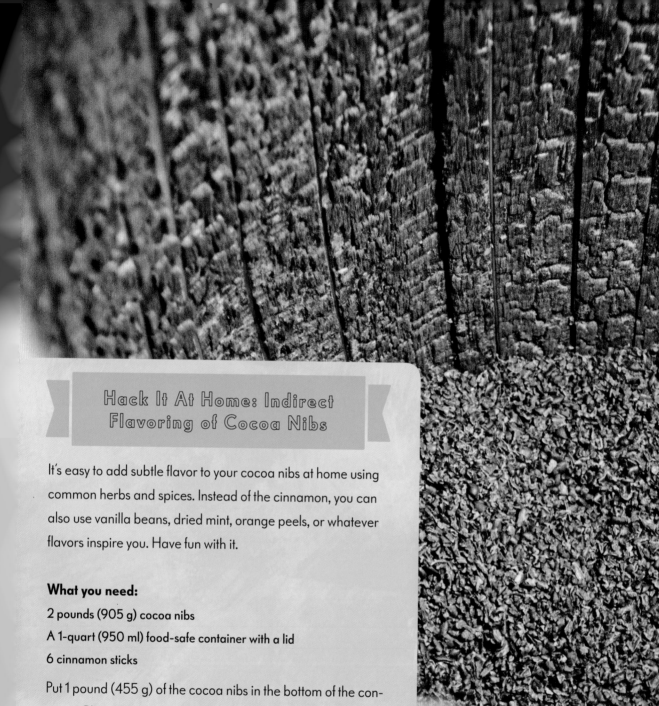

Hack It At Home: Indirect Flavoring of Cocoa Nibs

It's easy to add subtle flavor to your cocoa nibs at home using common herbs and spices. Instead of the cinnamon, you can also use vanilla beans, dried mint, orange peels, or whatever flavors inspire you. Have fun with it.

What you need:

2 pounds (905 g) cocoa nibs

A 1-quart (950 ml) food-safe container with a lid

6 cinnamon sticks

Put 1 pound (455 g) of the cocoa nibs in the bottom of the container. Place the cinnamon sticks on top of the nibs. Add the remaining 1 pound (455 g) nibs on top of the cinnamon sticks. Put the lid on the container and shake. Set in your kitchen cabinet or another safe spot for 2 to 3 weeks.

Remove the cinnamon. Now you have cinnamon-flavored cocoa nibs to use in your next batch of chocolate.

FLAVORING THE FAT IN CHOCOLATE

As we've learned, cocoa nibs are roughly half cocoa powder and half cocoa butter. That cocoa butter represents fat that lends itself tremendously to the transfer of flavor from other fragrant substances. I have infused cocoa nibs by leaving them in used bourbon barrels and rum barrels; storing them in airtight containers with vanilla or strong-smelling woods such as palo santo or cherry; or steaming them over simmering wine or herb-infused liquids. This strategy for flavoring cocoa nibs predates the invention of the chocolate bar itself. Sometime around 1680, Francesco Redi, a renowned Italian poet and scientist who was the physician to the Grand Duke of Tuscany, developed a chocolate beverage that was infused with the delicate scent of jasmine. His recipe called for placing cocoa nibs in a box and layering them with jasmine flowers. Every twenty-four hours, the contents of the box were to be fixed and new layer of nibs and flowers started. These steps were to be repeated for up to twelve days to get the desired jasmine flavor. Redi gave this recipe out only under strict instructions not to show it to anyone. Redi believed his discovery of flavoring the fat of cocoa beans with jasmine flowers to be significant, and he wanted no one to be able to replicate it. The recipe was eventually circulated after his death in 1697.

FLAVORING COCOA BUTTER

Another way I like to add flavor via fat in chocolate is by flavoring extra cocoa butter to then add to the chocolate later. This is another great way to add flavor to chocolate without adding texture. Powdered fruits and spices can be added to chocolate for flavor, but I find this to be problematic for two reasons. First, you're adding fiber to your chocolate, which is going to affect the texture of the finished chocolate. Extra refining or finding the right balance of added cocoa butter will need to be done to ensure you have a beautiful finished texture. Second, powdered spices in particular can have a very sharp and powerful flavor. This strong flavor can get in the way of the flavor of the cocoa beans you've carefully chosen.

By flavoring the fat via indirect aging or through added flavored cocoa butter, you're not adding texture to the chocolate, and you're going to still get those strong cocoa flavors from the beans you're using. Since the flavor you're infusing is being stored in the fat or the cocoa butter in both cases, and that fat stays solid until it gets to about human body temperature, the first flavors you'll taste when you eat chocolate that's been flavored this way are those of the cocoa solids. It is not until the cocoa butter begins to melt that your taste buds get hit with the second wave of flavor that's been locked into the fat by your infusion. Learning to layer flavors is really the core of the art of making flavored dark chocolates.

I find that the best flavors to infuse cocoa butter with come from teas and coffee. Both tea and coffee have finicky flavor compounds that can go south fast if the right times and temperatures aren't followed. This is especially true of teas in the *Camellia sinensis* species. These are all the teas derived from the tea plant, so all white, green, black, and oolong varieties of tea. Herbal teas tend to have more flexible rules for optimum flavor. As a result, tea and coffee should be infused at a relatively low temperature to avoid the transfer of bitter and astringent flavors. This is why I would avoid trying to steam cacao over boiling tea or coffee. Since cocoa butter melts at a low temperature, it is a perfect pairing for this type of infusion, and it's relatively simple to do it at home.

Making a cocoa butter infusion at home won't take a lot of time or effort, and it will make your kitchen smell great. Here are instructions for a simple coffee infusion that can be used in making chocolate or mixed into melted chocolate during baking. Also try this with Earl Grey tea or green tea. Play with the times and temperatures to find your ideal flavor.

What you need:
A small double boiler
3 ½ ounces (100 g) cocoa butter
6 tablespoons (50 g) coarse-ground coffee
A fine-mesh strainer or some cheesecloth

Heat the double boiler over medium heat with an inch or so of water in the bottom. Place the cocoa butter in the top part of the double boiler and cover. Let the cocoa butter melt completely into a liquid state that resembles vegetable oil. Reduce the heat to low.

Add the coffee to the cocoa butter and stir so it is completely coated with the cocoa butter. Put the lid on the double boiler and leave on low heat for 40 minutes to infuse.

Place the strainer over a bowl and pour the coffee and cocoa butter mixture through it, removing the coffee grounds.

TEMPERING CHOCOLATE

After chocolate is made, it is full of fat and sugar crystals. The fat of the cocoa butter present in your chocolate is polymorphic. This means that your cocoa butter can exist in many different crystalline forms. Cocoa butter has six different forms. The sixth and final form is the one you want to develop when tempering your chocolate. If the other forms take shape while your chocolate is hardening, it will negatively affect the texture and look of your chocolate bar.

If you've ever purchased a chocolate bar on a hot day and had it accidentally melt and then put it in your refrigerator to re-harden, you've probably noticed a white or gray blotchiness on the surface of the bar, and you may have noticed the presence of an unusually crumbly or chewy texture when you ate it. This is caused by fat bloom. Fat bloom is the unsuccessful attempt of the lower-form crystals to morph into crystal six. When you temper, you don't want any cocoa butter crystals lagging behind. If they do, they'll ruin the texture and appearance of your chocolate bar by attempting to appear like the other crystals. Getting all these fat crystals to act in unison is what tempering is all about. (Other materials that can be tempered include glass, steel, and cast iron. These are polymorphic materials just like cocoa butter and are tempered for various reasons; they just react under much more extreme temperatures than cocoa butter does.)

For chocolate to temper properly, all the cocoa butter crystals in the chocolate need to melt out completely. This happens around 120°F (49°C). When chocolate is tempered properly, it has a lovely shine to its appearance and a sharp snap when you break it. Additionally, it should melt slowly and evenly as it adjusts to the temperature inside your mouth. One of the things that makes chocolate such a sensual experience to consume is the way that the cocoa butter perfectly melts in your mouth like few other foods can. On the other hand, crumbly or chewy chocolate that melts unevenly in your mouth can be strange and unnerving, even if the taste of the chocolate is pleasant.

Tempering on a commercial scale is done with large machines that can heat and cool chocolate to the specific temperatures needed for the proper crystal formation in cocoa butter. These machines come in two types: batch temperers and continuous temperers.

Batch temperers: These machines melt out all the cocoa butter crystals and bring them through the cycle of temperatures needed to temper the chocolate once. This is done by heating and cooling water in coils in the walls of the machine until the chocolate is in temper, at which point it is all molded at once. This method is generally used for medium- to large-scale production.

Continuous temperers: These machines hold melted chocolate in a bowl at 120°F (49°C) and rapidly cool the chocolate as it circulates, continuously melting and re-tempering the chocolate. The advantage to this machine is that a portion of chocolate can be added to the machine at any time, in or out of a tempered state, and be quickly worked into tempered chocolate without breaking the machine's cycle. This type of machine is generally used for small-scale production, and also in large factories where a lot of re-melting and reworking of chocolate is happening.

Hack It at Home: Tempering

With a few simple tools and the time to pay attention to what's going on, you should be able to temper chocolate at home with no problems. There are two options for tempering at home: the seeding method and the slab method. The slab method requires that you have a large piece of marble sitting around, so I will teach you the seeding method. The seeding method uses a piece of already tempered chocolate (the "seed") to teach your untempered chocolate how to form crystal six. You want to make sure the room you're working in is no cooler than about 66°F (19°C) and no warmer than 79°F (26°C). Higher or lower ambient temperatures will make tempering very difficult, if not impossible.

What you need:

A double boiler

18 to 28 ounces (500 to 800 g) untempered dark chocolate

A digital or infrared thermometer

A spatula

2 small pieces tempered chocolate (about ⅓ ounce, or 8 g, total)

Set the double boiler over medium heat with an inch or so of water in the bottom and fill the top pot with the untempered chocolate. Stir the chocolate with the spatula as it melts, stirring until all of the chocolate reaches 120°F (49°C). It's important to take readings at different places in the pot to make sure all of the chocolate has reached the correct temperature. This is why I generally prefer an

infrared thermometer, as it allows you to take multiple readings quickly while you stir.

Once all the chocolate has reached the correct temperature, remove the top pot from the double boiler and turn off the stove (reserve the hot water in the bottom of the double boiler). Continue to stir the chocolate and monitor the temperature as it cools. When the chocolate reaches 98°F (37°C), stir in the tempered chocolate. This chocolate will slowly melt as your chocolate continues to cool, introducing your chocolate to the proper crystalline structure. Continue to stir.

After the tempered pieces have melted and mixed in, cool the chocolate to 85°F (29°C). It is important to keep stirring the chocolate continuously and to frequently scrape the sides of the pot with the spatula to ensure that none of the chocolate is cooling faster than the rest. Once your chocolate cools to the correct temperature, it will begin to thicken. Take the temperature of the water in the bottom of the double boiler; you need it to be around 88°F to 89°F (31°C to 32°C). If it is hotter than this, add cold water until it reaches this temperature. If it is colder, put it on the stove briefly to heat it to this temperature.

Put your 85°F (29°C) chocolate back over the hot water to ensure you hold the chocolate at this temperature for about 5 minutes. Place the double boiler back on the stove over low heat and slowly raise the temperature of the chocolate to 88°F (31°C). At this temperature, your chocolate will still be in temper, but it will be easier to work with.

Pour your chocolate into chocolate bar molds, or dip fruits or nuts into it, and let it cool. Take a deep breath—you tempered chocolate!

CHAPTER 4

CHOCOLATE RECIPES

MODERN-DAY OAXACA

The state of Oaxaca in Mexico is the modern-day archaeological site, so to speak, for culinary enthusiasts looking to taste the history of chocolate in the Americas. Oaxaca is a place that carried on the tradition of the sanctity of cacao into relatively recent history. As recently as the 1960s, people with Zapotec heritage in Oaxaca were often buried with a cacao pod to signify giving a gift to the gods in the afterlife. The tradition of drinking chocolate and making chocolate drinks in a traditionally indigenous manner has persisted in modern-day Oaxaca, whereas it has fallen off in other regions. If you walk into a market in Oaxaca, you're likely to be faced with five or six options of chocolate drinks: chocolate atole, tejate, champurrado, or simple chocolate with water or milk, to name a few.

In addition to chocolate drinks, you'll find a rich history of cuisine that uses chocolate, including many moles made with chocolate. These moles are used in stews, on enchiladas, and in other ways. It's a far cry from the primarily sweet uses that we typically associate with chocolate and cuisine. The markets in Oaxaca are filled with the sweet scents of chocolate, vanilla, cinnamon, and chile peppers, mixed with the savory aromas of grilled meat, cilantro, black pepper, and chile peppers (yes, chile peppers are both sweet and savory). The smoke-filled air and the energy in the markets bubble with the creativity and tradition of food that is completely deliberate and crafted with care. It feels like stepping back in time when you compare it to the generic scents and sounds of the modern supermarket.

The recipes in this book are not all Mexican in their origin, but they are inspired by the ideal set by Oaxaca, that chocolate can be something much more than a candy or a treat, that it can be part of your cuisine and your daily existence in a deeper way. I'm not a baker or a confectioner, but I am a chocolate maker who has spent a lot of time figuring out new ways to taste and experience chocolate. It is my hope that these recipes inspire you to think about chocolate differently and to share that experience with others.

TEJATE AND CHAMPURRADO

Despite how far we've come in the history of chocolate, many chocolate drinks continue to stand the test of time. Two of the most prevalent in the Oaxaca Valley are tejate and champurrado. These chocolate beverages are labor-intensive compared to the instant hot chocolate much of the world is used to today. These beverages have been around since pre-Colombian times. We're talking about culinary history that is nearly 1,000 years old.

Both these drinks have their roots in Aztec, Zapotec, and Mayan cultures. Both are served with a foam on the top. They both are ritually consumed at celebrations and special events. They both contain the mystique of being feminine in their energies. Traditionally, a woman always makes tejate or champurrado because only a woman possesses the right mix of energy and patience to extract the foam from the various ingredients. A man does not have the correct energy. I bought ingredients for tejate in Oaxaca and tried to make it myself, and couldn't. Instead of having a thick, luxurious foam on top of my creamy tejate, it was instead a mealy, chunky mess.

Tejate is specifically interesting because, unlike champurrado, it requires no specific tools, just a human fist. Also, tejate is nearly impossible to find outside of Oaxaca because the recipes and specific process behind making it are guarded by a union of tejate makers from San Andrés Huayapam, a small village in the hills outside Oaxaca City. This beverage is so important to regional culture that they want no one to be able to replicate it outside of their communities in a very specific region. It seems unbelievable that, in the twenty-first century in the age of social media and globalization, something can be protected this sacredly. Champurrado, on the other hand, is relatively easy to make at home, difficult to mess up, and the champurrado stick itself is somewhat of a common Mexican souvenir.

Here I've listed the ingredients for tejate and how the basic process of making it goes. It will be less of a traditional recipe because the ingredients and process involved are literally unknown to almost all of the world, but the ingredients and process do tell an important story of the ancient cultures of chocolate.

Champurrado was very much adopted by the Spanish and spread throughout Spain and the Spanish colonies, so recipes are prevalent.

SERVES 3 OR 4

FOR TEJATE:

White maize (corn)

Cacao beans

White cacao

Rosita de cacao

Mamey pits

Water

The white maize is prepared by cooking it with ash or limestone in a pot of water until softened. The cacao beans and white cacao (which is not cacao at all but a sister plant of cacao called *Theobroma bicolor*) are toasted on a round clay or cast-iron pan called a comal until the shells are brittle enough to be removed. The cacao and corn are then ground together with rosita de cacao flowers and presoaked/softened mamey pits on a stone metate or ground in a mechanical molino. This creates a brown dough-like substance.

The tejate dough is then place in a very large bowl. Slowly, a woman adds water to the mixture while kneading and churning it with her fist. Once the consistency of the mixture resembles that of porridge, the churning intensifies into something just shy of a beating. Water continues to be added in various deliberate stages. Eventually, the beating will begin to produce a chunky, fatty, white foam. At this point, more water is added, and a dried gourd is plunged into the mixture and raised high above the woman's head. The contents of the gourd are then poured in a 2- to 3-foot stream above the bowl and back into the main mixture. This step is repeated many times until an adequate foam is formed.

FOR CHAMPURRADO:

3 cups (705 ml) milk

2 tablespoons (28 g) panela or dark brown sugar

1 cinnamon stick

2 cups (475 ml) water

½ cup (70 g) masa (see page 106)

1 cup (175 g) chopped dark chocolate

Put the milk, panela, and cinnamon stick in a medium saucepan over medium-low heat. Cook until the sugar dissolves, about 10 minutes. Stir constantly to ensure you don't burn the milk. Turn off the heat and let the mixture rest.

Heat the water in another medium saucepan to just below a boil. Slowly whisk in the masa until it is smooth and contains no clumps.

Remove the cinnamon stick from the milk, and put the milk back over medium-low heat. Whisk in the water-masa mixture. Slowly whisk in the chocolate, allowing it to melt evenly. Once all the chocolate is melted and your champurrado is smooth, transfer to a large bowl.

Using a champurrado stick (which is inexpensive and easy to find online), aerate your champurrado by spinning the stick between your two palms. (You can also use a hand mixer to aerate your champurrado, but that's less fun and certainly less traditional.) Aerate until your liquid has developed a foam, and then serve immediately.

SIMPLE CHOCOLATE SAUCE

We all have fond memories of chocolate sauce. I remember mixing it into milk to make chocolate milk and drizzling it over ice cream to make an ice cream sundae. In winters growing up in Illinois and Massachusetts, we obviously used chocolate sauce to make hot chocolate after sledding or playing in the snow. Unfortunately, most commercially available chocolate sauces don't actually contain any chocolate. Instead, most contain either chocolate flavoring or cocoa powder, or if you're "lucky," both. In addition to not containing chocolate, commercial chocolate sauce is also chock-full of corn syrup and stabilizers. Here is a recipe for chocolate sauce that contains actual chocolate and is super-easy to make and store. This recipe contains a small amount of sunflower lecithin to prevent the cocoa butter in the chocolate from separating in the water. It's easy to find online or in a natural foods store.

MAKES 2 CUPS (475 ML)

1 cup (235 ml) water, preferably purified

1 cup (200 g) sugar

7 ounces (195 g) chocolate, coarsely chopped

½ teaspoon sunflower lecithin

Put the water and sugar in a small saucepan over medium-high heat. Allow the sugar to melt and the liquid to come to a boil. Keep it at a boil for 5 minutes. Remove the pan from the heat and slowly mix in the chocolate with a whisk. Whisk until the chocolate is fully melted and the mixture is smooth. Add the sunflower lecithin and continue to whisk until there is no separation in the liquid.

Pour into a jar and allow to cool. Stored in an airtight jar in the refrigerator, the sauce will keep for 3 to 4 weeks.

COCOA KAHLÚA

Kahlúa is a versatile liqueur that can perk up any party. It works well with both cold and hot drinks. It can work as a mix-in in an after-dinner coffee or as an ingredient in a dessert martini. Coffee liqueur is also easy to make from scratch at home. There are few things I love more than a good coffee and chocolate pairing. This liqueur is a bit more chocolaty than is traditional. This recipe is the set-it-and-forget-it type, and there's very little prep; patience is the main prerequisite. I'm pretty sure it'll be worth the wait. After you've made this liqueur once, play around with the quantities of each ingredient to find a blend you enjoy. I'm a big fan of experimentation in the kitchen.

MAKES ABOUT 8 CUPS (1.9 L)

3 cups (705 ml) freshly brewed coffee

3 cups (600 g) sugar

2 cups (475 ml) vodka

½ cup (120 ml) dark rum

½ cup (60 g) toasted cocoa nibs

2 vanilla beans, sliced lengthwise

Put the coffee and sugar in a large saucepan over medium heat. Stir until the sugar has fully dissolved in the coffee. Remove from the heat.

Once the mixture has cooled a bit, to just warm to the touch, mix in the vodka and rum.

For the final step, you'll need a bottle or two mason jars. If you're using just one vessel, put the nibs and vanilla beans in the bottle. If you're using two jars, simply split the ingredients equally between the jars.

Using a funnel, pour your liquid mixture into your vessel(s). Seal the bottle or jars and set aside for 3 to 4 weeks, after which point your liqueur will be ready to enjoy.

DRINKING CHOCOLATE

You can think of drinking chocolate as hot cocoa's grown-up cousin: sophisticated yet nostalgic, indulgent yet soothing. For my drinking chocolate, I like to use a combination of heavy cream and whole milk to make it rich yet approachable. The key for great drinking chocolate is a lot of chocolate. In this recipe, I add a little bit of chocolate sauce for sweetness, vanilla bean powder for a pop of flavor, and sea salt to enhance the chocolate flavor and for a bit of balance.

SERVES 4

2 cups (475 ml) whole milk

1 cup (235 ml) heavy cream

8 ounces (225 g) dark chocolate, chopped

¼ cup (60 ml) Simple Chocolate Sauce (page 94)

⅛ teaspoon vanilla bean powder

⅛ teaspoon sea salt

Combine the milk and heavy cream in a small saucepan over medium heat. Allow the mixture to come to a simmer, and reduce the heat to low. Stir in the chocolate slowly with a whisk until smooth. Add the chocolate sauce, vanilla bean powder, and sea salt, and stir until incorporated. Remove from the heat and serve.

CHÈVRE ET FÈVES ET PINOT NOIR

This recipe comes from Mark Bitterman, published cookbook author, owner of The Meadow and the Bitterman Salt Co., and culinary genius extraordinaire. Mark's stores in New York City and Portland, Oregon, have done an exceptional job of cultivating community around the finer things: salt, chocolate, and bitters. The Meadow has been a library of sorts for craft chocolate since before anyone was talking about bean-to-bar chocolate. This recipe combines chocolate, salt, wine, and cheese—in other words, things we all hold dear. It's perfect for a dinner party, or for a quiet, decadent night in.

SERVES 4

1 cup (120 g) cocoa nibs

1 log (8 ounces, or 225 g) fresh goat cheese

Pinot Noir salt, for sprinkling (or a finishing salt of your choice)

1 baguette, cut on the diagonal into ¼-inch (4 mm) slices

Spread half of the cocoa nibs across a shallow plate. Place the log of goat cheese on the nibs and pour the remaining nibs over the top.

Lightly roll the log in the nibs until it is well coated, then roll the log with more pressure to encrust the cheese with the nibs.

Set on a clean serving platter and sprinkle the log with the salt, allowing plenty of salt to scatter across the platter.

Arrange the slices of baguette around the cheese, over the scattered salt. To serve, cut a round of cheese from the log, place it on a slice of baguette, and top with a pinch of the salt.

COCOA NIB AND MELON SALAD

A nice fruity cocoa nib is a great addition to almost any salad. I know lots of people who add nibs to yogurt parfaits and smoothies, but not too many who add them to salads. They're great to use in place of or in addition to nuts and seeds, and they pair well with mild cheeses. I like adding them to salads where something other than lettuce is the star. Nibs are good with tomato salads such as panzanella or in a refreshing cucumber salad, but this is one of my favorite salads for using nibs. In the late summer, when honeydew and all types of other great lighter-flesh melons are in season in California, I make this frequently.

SERVES 4 TO 6

Half of a honeydew melon, seeded

2 to 3 ounces (55 to 85 g) ricotta salata cheese

2 tablespoons (15 g) cocoa nibs

½ tablespoon chopped fresh mint

1 tablespoon (20 g) wildflower honey

1 teaspoon balsamic vinegar

Salt and freshly ground black pepper

Cut the honeydew half into two pieces and slice each piece along the short side into ⅛-inch (3 mm) slivers. Arrange on a large platter or individual plates.

Using a handheld slicer or a knife, cut the cheese into paper-thin strips and arrange on the melon pieces.

Sprinkle the nibs and mint evenly across the melon and cheese. Drizzle the honey and vinegar all over the platter. Season with salt and pepper, which will enhance the sweetness of the melon. Serve immediately.

THAI COCONUT AND LEMONGRASS CHOCOLATE SOUP

Many flavors get talked about as being the most classic flavor combinations in the world: tomatoes and mozzarella, maple and bacon, caramel and sea salt. I've got a combination that I'm willing to toss into the conversation with those other classics: coconut milk and lemongrass. There's something about the sweet and creamy coconut with the slightly spicy, almost medicinal flavor of the lemongrass that, like Grandma's chicken soup, makes you feel like you're doing something right by your body. I've played around a lot with chocolate, coconut, and lemongrass combinations in various things, including truffles, chocolate bars, and brownies, but none are quite as healing as this soup. Serve this with rice noodles and steamed shrimp or braised chicken. For a one-dish vegetarian meal, add cubed tofu and snow peas at the same time you add the bell pepper and mushrooms.

SERVES 4

2 cups (475 ml) chicken broth

1¼ cups (295 ml) coconut milk

1 piece (4 inches, or 10 cm) lemongrass

½ tablespoon chopped fresh ginger

½ teaspoon salt

¼ teaspoon freshly ground black pepper

2 carrots, peeled and cut into ¼-inch (6 mm) rounds

½ yellow onion, diced

1 red bell pepper, diced

6 ounces (170 g) cremini mushrooms, sliced

¼ cup (60 ml) Simple Chocolate Sauce (page 94)

2 tablespoons (5 g) chopped fresh Thai basil, plus leaves for garnish

Combine the broth and coconut milk in a medium pot over medium heat. Slice the lemongrass into thin rounds and add to the pot, along with the ginger, salt, and pepper.

Bring to a simmer and then add the carrots and onions. Simmer for 10 minutes. Add the bell pepper and mushrooms and cook for 5 minutes more. Remove from the heat and stir in the chocolate sauce and basil. Garnish with basil leaves.

VARIATION:

For a dessert version, replace the chicken broth with ½ cup (120 ml) white wine. Allow the ginger and lemongrass to simmer for 15 minutes, then add ½ cup (120 ml) chocolate sauce (instead of ¼ cup, or 60 ml) with the basil. Serve with fresh fruit and biscotti for dipping.

RED MISO- AND CHOCOLATE-GLAZED VEGETABLES

I'm a huge fan of Japanese food. Japanese cuisine is almost entirely based around fermented foods. Soy sauce, katsuobushi, rice vinegar, and miso are all fermented foods that are staples of Japanese cuisine. Chocolate, being a fermented food, lends itself well to some of these flavors. We won't see a lot of Japanese recipes that involve chocolate, because chocolate is a relatively new phenomenon in Japan, and not really consumed at all until after World War II. I attended the Salon du Chocolat in Tokyo last year, and the absolute madness that was the Japanese reception to fine chocolate was breathtaking. As a new generation of Japanese chefs begin to bend the strict rules in Japanese cooking, I have no doubt that more chocolate will creep into pantry and be used as an ingredient in dishes. This dish is my attempt to insert chocolate into a traditional Japanese dish. Red miso is used all over Japan as the base for barbecue marinades and in cooked root vegetable dishes. Serve this over rice, if you like.

SERVES 4

¾ cup (175 ml) Simple Chocolate Sauce (page 94)

1 tablespoon (16 g) red miso paste

3 carrots, cut into ½-inch (1.2 cm) cubes

3 parsnips, peeled and cut into ½-inch (1.2 cm) cubes

4 jeweled yams, peeled and cut into ½-inch (1.2 cm) cubes

½ tablespoon toasted sesame oil

¼ teaspoon freshly ground black pepper

Preheat the oven to 375°F (190°C, or gas mark 5).

Put the chocolate sauce in a small saucepan and heat over medium heat for 5 minutes. Put the miso into a small bowl. Pour about a tablespoon of the warm chocolate sauce over the miso and stir until incorporated. Continue to add the chocolate sauce to the miso, a tablespoon at a time. Once all the chocolate sauce has been combined with the miso, let cool.

Place the vegetables in a gallon-size resealable plastic bag and pour the miso-chocolate mixture over them. Add the sesame oil and pepper. Seal the bag and shake it around until all the vegetables have been covered in the mixture. Place in the refrigerator to marinate for 6 hours.

Dump the vegetables (and the marinade) out of the bag onto a baking sheet, spreading them out evenly. Bake for 40 minutes, or until they are tender.

CHOCOLATE TORTILLAS

Corn and cacao are the two agricultural products that are ingrained in the fabric of Mesoamerica. There is literally a saying in Mexico, *"Sin maiz no hay paiz,"* which means "Without corn there is no country." Cacao is similar in that it was worshipped and used as currency for thousands of years in the same geographical area. I have a chef and chocolate maker I've been working with now for a number of years, Hector Hernandez, who is from a corn farm in Puebla, Mexico. We worked together on this special tortilla recipe, which combines two of our favorite things and two of the things most revered in Mesoamerica: corn and chocolate. When it comes to making tortillas, two things are important: 1) Buy great corn. There are a number of great resources online for dried heirloom corn. Do some research and find some exceptional corn. 2) Practice makes perfect. The more you make tortillas, the better they will be. Find yourself a tortilla-making buddy and get grinding.

MAKES 12 TO 15 TORTILLAS, WITH NIXTAMAL TO SPARE

FOR NIXTAMAL (CORN BASE):

2 quarts (1.9 L) plus 1 cup (235 ml) water, divided

1 tablespoon (9 g) ground lime (calcium hydroxide)

2 pounds (905 g) dried white corn

1 tablespoon (18 g) salt

FOR MASA (DOUGH):

3 cups (120 g) nixtamal, drained

½ cup (120 ml) water

1 tablespoon (15 ml) melted chocolate

2 tablespoons (12 g) unsweetened cocoa powder

EQUIPMENT:

Parchment or wax paper

Tortilla press

Grinder

To make the nixtamal: Combine 1 cup (235 ml) of the water and the ground lime in a bowl. Stir and let it fully dissolve. Let it sit for at least 20 minutes.

Meanwhile, put the remaining 2 quarts (1.9 L) water in a large pot and bring to a boil. Add the corn kernels, salt, and ground lime–water mixture, lower the heat, cover, and simmer for 2 hours, or until the corn has begun to soften but is not getting mushy.

Turn off the heat and allow the corn to soak in the water for a minimum of 8 hours.

To make the masa and tortillas: Drain the nixtamal in a colander, allowing all the water to fully drain away. Place the corn in a dry bowl.

Using a hand-crank grain mill or meat grinder, run 3 cups of the nixtamal through it. It will be tough to get cranking initially, but once you have it moving, the corn should flow through nicely.

Once the corn has been passed through the mill once, add the corn to a wet grinder slowly. As you add the corn slowly, add the water so that the grinder doesn't seize up. You can also play with the tension on the top of the grinder to ensure the corn stays in the grinder, because it will want to spin out. Put the lid on and allow the grinder to run for 10 minutes.

Remove the lid from the grinder. With the grinder running, add the melted chocolate, followed by the cocoa powder. Put the lid back on and let the grinder run for 5 minutes.

Turn off the grinder, remove the wheels, and scrape the masa stuck to the wheels into a bowl. Scrape the remainder of the masa from the grinder base into the bowl. Using your hands, work the masa to ensure all the ingredients are incorporated. When you have one large ball of masa with a consistent texture, you're ready to shape. Trace amounts of water may be added in this step if you're having trouble getting an even consistency. Be careful, however, because you want your masa to be thick, not too sticky or watery.

Form the masa into 1½-inch (3.7 cm) balls. Make sure they are pretty tightly packed. Have a bowl of water close by to dip your hands into if the balls are sticking to them.

Cut two pieces of plastic or parchment the size of your tortilla press. Place a ball of masa on the center of the press on one piece of plastic or parchment, place the other piece on top, and press down gently. Pull the press down halfway. Your tortillas should be about ⅛ inch (3 mm) thick. Don't make them any thinner or they will be too hard to cook.

Heat a clay or cast-iron comal or griddle over medium heat. Test the readiness of the pan by placing a small speck of your masa on the pan. If it sizzles and quickly releases from the surface, it's ready. If it sticks to the pan and doesn't release within a few seconds, you need to let the pan heat for a few more minutes.

Carefully place a tortilla on the comal and allow it to cook for a minute or two, then flip it and cook for a minute or two longer. It's best to cook tortillas with a friend or two so that you can press and cook quickly. It's difficult to press a bunch of tortillas and set them aside, as they basically need to be cooked immediately following pressing. Also, it's a whole lot of fun making tortillas, and you want to make sure you share that experience with friends. Stack your tortillas up as you cook them, and cover them with a clean kitchen towel. Your tortillas will stay fresh for 2 to 3 days. After that, if you have leftovers, cut them into triangles and fry them into tortilla chips.

VARIATIONS
During the grinding phase, add ½ cup (120 ml) cranberry juice instead of the water. Omit the melted chocolate and cocoa powder. This will turn your tortillas red instead of brown.

Or, blend up a roasted poblano chile and a jalapeño and add them instead of the chocolate ingredients to turn your tortillas green and give them a mild, pleasant heat.

CRISPY CHOCOLATE CARNITAS

Carnitas, or really pulled pork of any kind, is the ideal party food. It feeds a lot of people and can be served on rolls or tortillas. When I make carnitas, I like to give the dish just a hint of heat, and I like to incorporate chocolate. Pork and chocolate is my favorite sinful combination. Carnitas is also my go-to choice when I try a new taqueria. I've found that you can tell a lot about the quality of a taqueria based on the balance of moistness and crispiness contained in their carnitas. If the carnitas have a light crunch, but then melt in your mouth after you sink your teeth into them, then the taqueria cares a lot about the quality of the food they serve. Let's try our hand at it, shall we? Let's see if we can find that balance.

SERVES 6 TO 8

1 teaspoon salt

1 teaspoon freshly ground black pepper

¼ teaspoon ground ancho chile or Mexican chili powder

¼ teaspoon ground cumin

1 boneless pork butt (4 pounds, or 1.8 kg)

Juice of 2 limes

4 garlic cloves, smashed

1 jalapeño, seeds removed and sliced

1 dried guajillo chile, sliced

1 tablespoon (15 ml) Simple Chocolate Sauce (page 94)

Chocolate Tortillas (page 106), for serving

Roasted onions, tomatillos, and poblano chiles, for serving (optional)

Combine the salt, pepper, ground chile, and cumin in a small bowl. Wash the pork butt and place it on a rimmed baking sheet, fat side up. Rub in the spices. Cover with aluminum foil and put the pork in the fridge overnight, or for 8 to 10 hours.

Preheat the oven to 275°F (140°C, or gas mark 1). Uncover the pork and using a brush, baste liberally with the lime juice. Cover again with foil and place on a rack in the middle of the oven. Bake for 8 hours, until the meat falls apart when you poke it with a fork, basting with lime juice every 2 hours.

Remove the pork from the oven and let rest on a cooling rack for 30 minutes. Using two forks, pull the meat apart into shreds, letting the shreds fall and soak in the rendered fat on the bottom of the baking sheet.

Using a turkey baster, remove about ½ cup (120 ml) fat from the bottom of the baking sheet. Put the fat into a large cast-iron skillet and place on the stove over high heat. Add the garlic and chiles to the skillet and cook. When the fat is hot and the garlic has begun to brown, slowly and carefully add the pork. Cook for 8 to 10 minutes, stirring occasionally. If you have too much pork to fit in your skillet, cook it in batches. Simply use a skimmer to remove the cooked pork and place it into a serving bowl, and repeat. After you've cooked all the pork, drizzle the chocolate sauce over it and toss to combine. Serve hot, in the tortillas and with the toppings of your choice.

TWO MOLES

Mole poblano is the unofficial official dish of Mexico. It's a complex sauce often prepared with chicken or turkey. If you talk to any Mexican chef, chances are they have their own secret recipe for mole poblano. Finding a recipe for this dish is not hard, but finding the origin of it is another story. This dish likely didn't originate from pre-conquest Mayan culture, though it is prevalent in native Mesoamerican culture today. It's an old dish that is a mixture of indigenous Mesoamerican and Spanish cooking. Popular legend has it that the nuns of the convent of Santa Rosa in Puebla were responsible for its creation. In preparation for a visit from the Archbishop, the nuns scraped together what little they had to make a special sauce to serve with a turkey. When the sauce of chiles, spices, and old bread was bubbling, the legend goes that chocolate fell off the shelf and into the sauce. The Archbishop loved the sauce so much that the nuns continued to make it on special occasions, and word of the sauce spread throughout Puebla. There are numerous legends of similar ilk.

Moles are most broadly defined as a sauce made from chile peppers; some contain chocolate, and some do not. There are dozens of varieties of mole all over Mexico, but the states of Puebla and Oaxaca argue over which one is the capital of mole. Here are recipes for two different moles that contain chocolate. The method is the same for bath.

BLACK MOLE MAKES ABOUT 4 QUARTS (3.8 L); RED MOLE MAKES ABOUT 2 QUARTS (1.9 L)

FOR BLACK MOLE:

9 mulato chiles

7 ancho chiles

7 pasilla chiles

2 chipotle chiles

½ cup (113 g) pork lard, divided

½ cup (72 g) sesame seeds

2 tablespoons (8 g) pepitas (pumpkin seeds)

1 teaspoon cumin seeds

1 teaspoon coriander seeds

1 teaspoon freshly ground black pepper

½ teaspoon dried thyme

½ teaspoon ground cinnamon

½ teaspoon ground cloves

½ cup (80 g) diced onion

Preheat the oven to 300°F (150°C, or gas mark 2). Remove the stems and seeds from the chiles, reserve the seeds, spread the chiles on a baking sheet, toast the chiles in the oven for 10 minutes.

Melt 2 tablespoons (28 g) of the lard in a medium skillet. Add the sesame seeds, pepitas, and whole and ground spices and cook until the sesame seeds start to brown. Remove the seeds and spices from the skillet, add another 2 tablespoons (28 g) lard, and brown the onions and garlic in the fat. Add the reserved chile seeds and raisins and cook until the seeds turn brown.

After the toasted chiles have cooled, put them in a water bath to rehydrate for 1 hour.

Set aside the chocolate and salt, and blend all of the other dry ingredients in a blender, along with the chiles, into a barely moist paste.

4 garlic cloves, peeled

2 tablespoons (18 g) raisins

2 tablespoons (18 g) roasted peanuts

2 tablespoons (18 g) roasted almonds

1 slice white bread, cubed

1 ½ corn tortillas

1 saltine cracker

2 ounces (55 g) dark chocolate

1 tablespoon (18 g) salt

1 yellow plantain, sliced and panfried

2 Roma tomatoes, roasted

2 ½ quarts (2.4 L) chicken broth

FOR RED MOLE:

6 ancho chiles

8 guajillo chiles

½ cup (113 g) pork lard, divided

¼ cup (36 g) sesame seeds

2 tablespoons (8 g) pepitas (pumpkin
    seeds)

¼ cup (36 g) roasted almonds

1 star anise pod

1 cinnamon stick

5 allspice berries

1 teaspoon epazote

½ teaspoon dried oregano

1 Spanish onion, diced

6 garlic cloves, chopped

¼ cup (37 g) raisins

2 ounces (55 g) dark chocolate

½ tablespoon salt

1 corn tortilla

2 tomatoes, roasted

3 tomatillos, roasted

4 cups (950 ml) chicken broth

Heat 2 tablespoons (28 g) of the lard in a large skillet over medium heat and lightly fry the paste, adding water as needed to prevent the paste from burning. Add the chocolate and salt. After the chocolate has melted, cook for 30 minutes, stirring constantly so you don't burn the mixture.

Heat the remaining 2 tablespoons (28 g) lard in a large pot over medium heat. Add the roasted tomatoes and either the plantains or the tomatillos, depending on which mole you are making. Reduce the juices for about 15 minutes. Blend them in the blender until smooth, and return them to the pot. Add the broth and fried mole paste and stir constantly while cooking over medium heat for 30 minutes.

Now you can boil or roast a chicken or turkey, pull the meat off the bones, and finish cooking it in your mole. Serve it with chocolate tortillas, or with beans and rice.

CHOCOLATE STOUT ROLLS

Chocolate malt is a type of malted barley with an extremely aromatic nose. The name of this malt comes from the fact that it smells and tastes like chocolate, even though no chocolate is used in the processing of it. Typically, chocolate stout beers contain a percentage of this type of malt to infuse them with the aroma and taste of chocolate. Oftentimes these beers are also aged with cocoa nibs or contain small amounts of chocolate to increase the chocolate flavor. I love using these types of beers in baking to infuse bread, or in this case oatmeal rolls, with the slightest hint of chocolate. These rolls pair well with my short ribs (see page 118).

MAKES 8 TO 10 ROLLS

4 cups (548 g) bread flour, divided

1 ¾ cups (140 g) rolled oats, plus more for topping

1 bottle (12 ounces, or 355 ml) chocolate stout

2 teaspoons active dry yeast

2 teaspoons salt

5 tablespoons (100 g) molasses

2 tablespoons (28 g) butter, melted

¾ cup (175 ml) milk, divided

1 large egg

1 tablespoon (13 g) sugar

Combine 1 cup (137 g) of the flour, the oats, and stout in a large bowl and stir until fully mixed. Allow to rest for 45 minutes.

Pour the mixture into the bowl of a stand mixer and use the kneading hook to combine the remaining flour, yeast, salt, molasses, and ½ cup (120 ml) milk.

At this point, the dough will be very loose and liquid, so allow your stand mixer to run for 10 to 12 minutes. You'll know when the dough is getting close if it begins to become elastic and slap the sides of the bowl when it's turned by the hook. When it does this, allow it a few more turns to form a circular ball around the hook and pull away from the sides.

Coat your hands with vegetable oil and transfer the dough to another bowl. Cover and allow to rest overnight so the dough rises.

Dump the dough onto an oiled baking sheet or clean work surface and, with well-oiled hands, press on the dough to release any air pockets that may have formed. Roll up the dough and portion it into 8 baseball-size rolls, about 5 ounces (140 g) each.

Arrange on a baking sheet about 3 inches (7.5 cm) apart, cover, and set aside for 1 ½ hours to let the dough rise once again. Preheat the oven to 400°F (200°C, or gas mark 6).

Whisk the egg with the remaining ¼ cup (60 ml) milk in a small bowl. Brush the tops of the rolls with the egg wash. Sprinkle oats on top of your rolls and bake for 20 minutes. Reduce the oven temperature to 350°F (180°C, or gas mark 4) and bake for an additional 10 minutes.

COCOA NIB SHORT RIB AND HONEY-ROASTED PEACH SANDWICHES ON CHOCOLATE STOUT ROLLS

These decadent and delicious sandwiches will surely impress party guests. Cocoa nibs are a great secret ingredient to use in red meat rubs. They pack so much flavor into such a tiny morsel, and they pair well with winter spices like cinnamon and allspice. A chocolate demi-glace is decadence at its finest, almost like a meaty ganache, if you will. Roasted or grilled pitted fruits like peaches, nectarines, and plums add just the right amount of natural sweetness to all kinds of recipes for stews, casseroles, and yes, even sandwiches.

MAKES 6 SANDWICHES

FOR SHORT RIBS:

1 tablespoon (8 g) cocoa nibs

1 teaspoon salt

¼ teaspoon freshly ground black pepper

¼ teaspoon ground chile pepper

⅛ teaspoon ground cinnamon

⅛ teaspoon ground allspice

4 pounds (1.8 kg) bone-in short ribs (2 or 3 pieces)

1 cup (235 ml) water

FOR PEACHES:

2 peaches, halved and pitted

1 teaspoon honey

¼ teaspoon salt

¼ teaspoon freshly ground black pepper

FOR DEMI-GLACE:

2 tablespoons (28 ml) rendered fat from ribs

2 tablespoons (28 ml) Simple Chocolate Sauce (page 94)

6 chocolate Stout Rolls (page 117)

To make the short ribs: Combine the nibs, salt, black pepper, chile pepper, cinnamon, and allspice in a food processor and pulse until fully mixed. Coat the short ribs with the mixture, place on a rimmed baking sheet, cover, and refrigerate overnight or for about 12 hours.

Preheat the oven to 325°F (165°C, or gas mark 3). Remove the short ribs from the refrigerator and let them come close to room temperature. Pour the water onto the bottom of a large baking dish and place a wire rack in the baking dish. Put the short ribs on the rack and cover with foil. Place in the oven and roast for 2 ½ hours, or until the meat begins to pull away from the bones.

Remove the foil, increase the oven temperature to 425°F (220°C, or gas mark 7), and roast for 20 minutes more. Remove from the oven and allow the meat to rest for at least 15 minutes. Leave the oven on for the peaches.

Cut the meat away from the bones and set aside, covered.

To make the peaches: Place the peach halves in a small cast-iron pan or pie plate with the skin side down. Coat the tops of the peaches with the honey and sprinkle with the salt and pepper. Place in the oven and roast for 15 minutes. Remove, allow to cool, and slice.

To make the demi-glace: Put the fat in a small saucepan over low heat and slowly whisk in the chocolate sauce, allowing each drizzle to incorporate before adding more.

To make the sandwiches: Cut the short ribs into ¼-inch (6 mm) slices. Cut the rolls in half. Arrange 4 or 5 slices of short ribs, followed by 4 or 5 slices of peaches, on the bottom of each roll. Drizzle a substantial amount of chocolate demi-glace over the peaches, add the roll tops, and enjoy with your friends. Serve with a dark beer, like a stout or porter.

COCOA NIB PAPPARDELLE WITH WILD MUSHROOM CREAM SAUCE

This recipe was inspired by Baroque-era Italians, who decided that they didn't care what the Spanish or anyone else thought, they were going to experiment with chocolate in their cuisine. There is evidence that chocolate pappardelle was in fact a dish that was made for a short period in Northern Italy. This dish likely consisted of a sauce that contained chocolate, whereas my version contains finely ground cocoa nibs in the pasta dough. This dish takes a little bit of patience and an attention to detail, but the result is an impressive use of cocoa as a strictly savory ingredient.

SERVES 4

FOR PASTA:

½ cup (60 g) cocoa nibs

2 cups (250 g) unbleached all-purpose flour

½ teaspoon salt

3 large eggs

1 tablespoon (15 ml) water, if needed

Olive oil, as needed

FOR SAUCE:

1 tablespoon (14 g) butter

1 shallot, minced

8 ounces (225 g) wild mushrooms

½ teaspoon salt

¼ teaspoon freshly ground black pepper

½ cup (120 ml) white wine

1 cup (235 ml) heavy cream

Chopped fresh basil or chives, for garnish

To make the pasta: Put the nibs in the freezer overnight. Remove and pulse them in a food processor till they're about one-quarter of their original size. It's important to pulse instead of blend, to prevent the nibs from releasing cocoa butter.

Put the flour in a large bowl and add the nibs and salt. Mix together until fully incorporated. Using your hands, make a well in the center of the mixture. Crack the eggs into the well you created. Combine the eggs and dry mixture gently with a fork.

If your dough is very dry, work in water ½ tablespoon at a time until the dough comes together. You shouldn't need more than 1 tablespoon (15 ml) water. Knead the dough on a floured surface for about 5 minutes. Put it in a covered bowl and refrigerate for 30 minutes.

Take the dough out of the fridge and cut it into quarters. Roll out the dough in a pasta maker or with a rolling pin. When the dough starts to get thin, some pieces of nib may tear the dough. Remove those pieces and repair the dough. It is likely you'll have to roll and rework the dough three or four times to remove all the larger nib pieces. If you don't remove them, they will continue to tear your dough. On the final roll, try to get your dough to about the thickness of two sheets of paper.

Once the dough is rolled, run it through your pasta maker on the thickest noodle cutter you have, or cut your rolled dough into strips that are about ½-inch (1.2 mm) thick.

Bring a large pot of water to a boil. Cook half of the noodles for 2 minutes. When you remove the noodles, using a skimmer, immediately toss them in a small amount of olive oil to prevent sticking. Repeat this with the rest of the noodles.

To make the sauce: Melt half of the butter in a medium skillet over medium-low heat. Sweat the shallots for 5 minutes, then add the mushrooms, the rest of the butter, and the salt and pepper. When the mushrooms have begun to soften (after about 5 minutes), add the wine and increase the heat to medium. Cook for 5 minutes.

Slowly swirl in the cream. Cook for 10 minutes while stirring. Be sure to lower the heat if the cream looks like it is going to start to boil.

Pour the sauce over the pasta and toss to combine. Serve with a sprinkle of fresh basil.

COCOA JERK CHICKEN

The culture of the West Indies is one of the most prominent cultures in Brooklyn. As a result, Jamaican, Trinidadian, and St. Lucian markets and restaurants line long stretches of Fulton Street in the north, and parts of Nostrand and Flatbush Avenues as you go farther south. It's a rich cuisine developed from a mashing of cultures from all over the globe, the perfect staple for a city like New York. Roti, double doubles, rice and peas, stewed yams, cassava bread: These foods are a fabric of the New York culinary scene. Being that I'm someone who enjoys the spicier things in life, my favorite of these foods is jerk chicken. Jerk spice made its way from West Africa to the Caribbean (Jamaica specifically) and the later addition of Scotch bonnet peppers is what gives it its distinctively island flare. The warm spices that are so important to the dish lend themselves to chocolate as well. When I make jerk chicken, I like to add cocoa, to give it my own chocolaty spin. And it makes sense, since cacao is an agricultural staple of the West Indies. Trinidad and Tobago is home to the largest cacao seed bank in the world.

SERVES 4

5 garlic cloves, chopped

1 or 2 Scotch bonnet chiles

1 ½ tablespoons (9 g) minced fresh ginger

3 tablespoons (39 g) coconut palm sugar

2 tablespoons (12 g) unsweetened cocoa powder

1 tablespoon (18 g) salt, or to taste

1 tablespoon (6 g) freshly ground black pepper

½ tablespoon ground allspice

½ teaspoon ground nutmeg

¾ cup (175 ml) pineapple or orange juice

Juice of 1 lime

1 tablespoon (15 ml) soy sauce

1 tablespoon (15 ml) canola or vegetable oil

½ yellow or Spanish onion, chopped

1 whole chicken, cut into quarters

2 cinnamon sticks

Combine the garlic, chiles, ginger, sugar, cocoa powder, salt, black pepper, allspice, nutmeg, juices, and soy sauce in a blender and pulse until it turns into a wet paste.

Heat the oil in a Dutch oven over medium heat. Sauté the onions until they start to brown. Add the chicken, the wet jerk paste, and the cinnamon sticks and cover the pot. Bring to a simmer over medium heat, then reduce the heat to low and cook for 1 ½ to 2 hours, until the chicken meat begins to pull away from the bones. Meanwhile, preheat the oven to 450°F (230°C, or gas mark 8).

Carefully remove the chicken from the Dutch oven and arrange skin-side up on a baking sheet. Brush the chicken with the paste from the bottom of the Dutch oven. Place in the oven and roast for 8 to 10 minutes, until the skin begins to brown.

SERVING NOTE:
Serve with rice and peas to soak up your spicy and delicious jerk paste. Slice some green cabbage into ¾-inch (2 cm) wedges and serve on the side for snacking when you need to cool your mouth from the heat of the dish.

CHOCOLATE PASTA DOUGH

There are few things that are more fun in the kitchen than making homemade pasta. It is truly an activity where creativity is king. Some of my fondest memories of the early days of dating my wife, Catherine, revolve around making homemade pasta together. Making pasta is a truly collaborative activity in the kitchen, and if you make a mistake, it's relatively easy to just start over. The addition of cocoa powder to pasta dough colors it a gorgeous mahogany brown and adds a roasty, bittersweet complexity to the dough that makes it great to use in both savory dishes and fun dessert pastas. I recommend picking up a hand pasta crank. You should be able to easily pick a basic one up for under $30. If you don't have one and want to try making pasta anyway, an empty wine bottle or a rolling pin and a knife or cookie cutter for cutting will do. So let hours of fun ensue.

MAKES 1 POUND (455 G)

3 large eggs, beaten

1 ¾ cups (220 g) unbleached all-purpose flour

1 ½ tablespoons (25 ml) olive oil

1 tablespoon (18 g) salt

Water, as needed

2 tablespoons (12 g) unsweetened cocoa powder, plus more for dusting and kneading

See suggested fillings, page 128

Put the eggs, flour, olive oil, and salt in a medium bowl. Using a stand mixer or your elbow grease, knead together until smooth, 5 to 6 minutes for a mixer or longer if kneading by hand. Add up to 1 tablespoon (15 ml) water if your dough isn't incorporating. Continue to knead while slowly adding in the cocoa powder until your dough has turned an even brown color.

For hand rolling: Dust a clean work surface with cocoa powder and press a golf ball–size ball of dough into a flat pancake. Dust the top of the dough disk with a generous amount of cocoa powder to prevent sticking and cover with a sheet of plastic wrap or waxed paper. Roll out with a rolling pin or empty wine bottle until you've gotten your desired thickness. Your dough may crack or get thinner in some areas than others; this is okay. Fold the dough over and start again. It's possible you didn't knead aggressively enough, so now you're using your rolling stage as an additional kneading stage.

Rolling your own tortellini: Rolling your own tortellini can be a fun and challenging endeavor. I'm all for group activities in the kitchen. Any time you can sit down and enjoy a meal that many hands came together to prepare, it's a special time. This useful step-by-step guide should get you well on your way to rolling your own chocolate tortellini with friends and family.

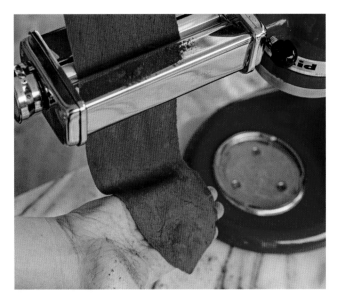

Grab the rolled chocolate dough and put it on a well-dusted work surface. I prefer to dust with cocoa powder, but flour will do just fine as well. Cut circles from your dough using a 2-inch (5 cm) round cookie cutter. Any remaining dough can be pressed back together into a ball and re-rolled.

Place a ½-teaspoon dollop of the filling of your choice in the center of your round, flat dough pieces.

Dip your index finger into a bowl of water and paint a ring on the edge of the dough using your wet finger.

Fold over one side of the dough circle as if to make a taco shape. Lightly press the wet edges of the dough together to form a seal. What you have should resemble an understuffed half-moon pillow. If your filling is coming out of the edges, you used too much. You can attempt to remove some and start over with the same circle of dough.

Place one of your pinky fingers in the middle of your dough pillow. Dip the index finger of your other hand in the bowl of water and wet one corner of the dough pillow. Fold the other corner around your pinky and attach the back end of that corner to the wet corner. Press firmly, but gently, to seal.

Stand up the dough roll and press down on the top so that the edges curl over the filled center. If you did it right, at this point you should have no problem recognizing your creation as tortellini. Repeat until you have all the tortellini you desire, or until you run out of dough, whichever comes first.

THREE TORTELLINI FILLINGS

After you've made your chocolate pasta dough, you're going to want to have something to fill it with. Here are three versatile options that go great with chocolate pasta dough. You can follow these recipes, or get creative and make your own. As a general rule, a solid balance of salty and sweet will pair well with your unsweetened chocolate pasta dough. These fillings work equally well if you'd rather make ravioli.

FOR LEMON RICOTTA FILLING:

1 cup (250 g) fresh ricotta cheese, drained

1 large egg

Zest of 1 lemon

¼ teaspoon salt

¼ teaspoon freshly ground black pepper

⅛ teaspoon ground nutmeg

Whip the ricotta and egg in a bowl until smooth. Add the lemon zest, salt, pepper, and nutmeg and stir to combine. Cover and refrigerate until ready to use.

MAKES 1 ½ CUPS (375 G)

FOR SPANISH PAPRIKA AND NIB LAMB RAGÙ FILLING:

3 tablespoons (45 ml) olive oil, divided

½ large onion, diced

2 garlic cloves, crushed

2 lamb shanks (1 pound, or 455 g, each)

¼ teaspoon salt

¼ teaspoon freshly ground black pepper

1 cup (235 ml) chicken broth

1 cinnamon stick

¼ cup (45 g) chopped roasted red peppers

½ teaspoon Spanish paprika

¼ cup (30 g) cocoa nibs

Heat 2 tablespoons (28 ml) of the olive oil in a medium saucepan over medium-high heat. Add the onion and garlic and sauté for a few minutes to soften them. Push them to the sides of the pan and add the lamb shanks, the remaining 1 tablespoon (15 ml) oil, the salt, and the pepper. Cook for 6 to 8 minutes, until the shanks begin to brown.

Lower the heat to medium and add the broth and cinnamon stick. Cover and simmer for 1 hour.

Remove the lid add the roasted red peppers and paprika. Simmer, uncovered, for an additional 30 minutes or until the liquid has mostly cooked off and the meat has pulled away from the bones.

Using a fork, pull all the meat away from the bones and remove the bones from the pot. Allow the meat and peppers to cool. Transfer to a bowl and mix in the cocoa nibs. Cover and refrigerate until ready to use.

MAKES 2 CUPS (455 G)

FOR CHERRY TAPENADE AND SOUR CREAM FILLING:

1 cup (155 g) pitted cherries

1 cup (100 g) pitted kalamata olives

¼ cup (35 g) pine nuts

1 tablespoon (15 ml) olive oil

½ teaspoon salt

½ teaspoon sugar

½ cup (115 g) sour cream

Put the cherries, olives, pine nuts, olive oil, salt, and sugar in a food processor and pulse into a chunky mixture. Scrape the ingredients into a bowl, add the sour cream, and mix with a spatula. Refrigerate until ready to use.

MAKES 3 CUPS (450 G)

LEMON RICOTTA-FILLED CHOCOLATE TORTELLINI IN BONE BROTH WITH MINT PESTO

It's time to turn your homemade tortellini into a show-stopping dish. There's nothing quite as rich and delicious as a beef-bone broth. Its comforting and hearty flavor makes it the perfect partner to stand up to the strong flavors of chocolate pasta. The key to a great beef-bone broth is great beef bones. This is not dissimilar to great chocolate: When the raw ingredient being used to make something is of exceptional quality, with the right technique, the end product will be something of exceptional quality. Other beef bones will do, but I prefer to use uncut marrow bones. Patience with these bones is the key. The longer you let them cook, the more delicious marrow flavor will seep out into your broth.

SERVES 4

FOR BONE BROTH:

5 pounds (2.3 kg) beef marrow bones

½ tablespoon salt

2 tablespoons (28 ml) olive oil

1 yellow onion, chopped

2 quarts (1.9 L) water

2 carrots, peeled and chopped

2 celery stalks, chopped

Salt and freshly ground black pepper

FOR TORTELLINI:

20 Chocolate Tortellini with Lemon Ricotta Filling (pages 124 and 128)

1 teaspoon olive oil

FOR PESTO:

½ cup (48 g) chopped fresh mint

¼ cup (25 g) chopped scallions (green parts only)

2 tablespoons (18 g) pine nuts

To make the bone broth: Preheat the oven to 400°F (200°C, or gas mark 6). Arrange the bones on a baking sheet and sprinkle with the salt. Put in the oven and roast for 45 minutes.

Heat the olive oil in a large pot over medium heat. Add the onions sauté until they start to turn brown. Add the bones, water, carrots, and celery. Raise the heat to high and bring to a boil. Reduce the heat to a simmer and cover. Simmer for 3 hours. Remove the lid and cook for 1 hour more so that the broth reduces.

Turn off the heat and pick up one of the bones with a set of tongs. If it looks like most of the marrow has rendered, your broth is done. Season with salt and pepper to taste. If the bones still contain a lot of marrow, you may elect to cook the broth longer to extract all that collagen goodness.

To make the tortellini: Bring a large pot of salted water to a boil. Gently drop in the tortellini. They should sink to the bottom of the pot. In 2 to 3 minutes, they will rise and start floating. When this happens, they're done. Remove them and toss in the olive oil to prevent them from sticking together.

To make the pesto: Combine the mint, scallions, pine nuts, olive oil, lemon juice, salt, and pepper in a food processor and blend until smooth. Put the mixture into a bowl or a squeeze bottle.

2 tablespoons (28 ml) olive oil

1 teaspoon fresh lemon juice

½ teaspoon salt

¼ teaspoon freshly ground black pepper

Portion the broth into bowls, evenly divide the tortellini between the bowls, and top with a dollop or a squiggle of the pesto. Serve immediately.

FLOURLESS CARDAMOM CHOCOLATE CAKE

Growing up, whenever we had family or special friends over for dinner, my mother would make a flourless chocolate cake. Her secret was adding a lot of chocolate, which coincidentally is a great secret. I can't help but get nostalgic for family meals and loved ones whenever I make or eat a flourless chocolate cake. I've added my own secret ingredient to the family recipe: cardamom. Cardamom tastes great with chocolate and can be infused into butter very easily because of its fragrant aroma. However, you may choose to infuse your cake with hibiscus, chile peppers, herbs, or something else entirely. You do you.

SERVES 8

12 ounces (340 g) chocolate, coarsely chopped

½ cup (112 g) butter

8 cardamom pods, cracked

5 large eggs, separated

1 ½ teaspoons sugar

1 teaspoon hot water

SERVING NOTE:

Drizzle Simple Chocolate Sauce (page 94) over the top of the cake while it's still in the pan. Or combine 1 ½ tablespoons (9 g) cocoa powder and 1 ½ tablespoons (11 g) confectioners' sugar in a bowl with ½ teaspoon ground cardamom and sift this over the top of the cake after you have removed it from the pan.

Preheat the oven to 425°F (220°C, or gas mark 7) and arrange a rack in the middle position.

Melt the chocolate in the top of a double boiler over low heat. Keep warm.

Melt the butter in a small saucepan over low heat. When the butter has melted, add the cracked cardamom pods, shells and all. Turn off the heat and let the pods steep in the butter for 10 minutes, stirring occasionally.

Pour the butter mixture into a small strainer set over the melted chocolate. Stir the butter and chocolate mixture until fully incorporated. Remove the chocolate-butter mixture from the stove and allow to cool for 5 minutes.

Add the egg yolks to the chocolate-butter mixture and lightly whip them in.

In a separate bowl, whip the egg whites, sugar, and hot water together until the egg whites form thick peaks.

Add about one-quarter of the egg whites to the chocolate mixture and whip them in. Gently fold the remaining egg whites into the chocolate mixture.

Pour the batter into a 9-inch (23 cm) springform pan and bake for 15 minutes. Let cool for 5 minutes before serving.

CHOCOLATE STOUT COOKIES

These crunchy, chocolaty cookies are delicious on their own, or go all out and fill them with a cream filling, like a whoopie pie. I also like to break them up and use them as the crust for pies and cheesecakes (see page 138). Everyone needs a great cookie recipe to bust out when needed, and this is mine. This again incorporates a touch of chocolate stout for depth of flavor, just like the dinner rolls (see page 117).

MAKES ABOUT 25 COOKIES

1 ½ cups (145 g) unsweetened cocoa powder, plus more for dusting

1 ½ cups (188 g) unbleached all-purpose flour

¼ teaspoon salt

1 cup (225 g) butter, softened

2 cups (400 g) sugar

½ cup (120 ml) chocolate stout

2 large eggs

¼ teaspoon vanilla bean powder

Sift the cocoa powder, flour, and salt together in a large bowl.

In a stand mixer or with a handheld mixer, cream the butter and sugar. While mixing slowly, pour in the stout, then add the eggs one at a time, mixing until incorporated. Sprinkle in the vanilla powder and mix until incorporated.

Transfer the dough to a bowl and cover with plastic wrap. Place in the refrigerator for about 30 minutes.

Preheat the oven to 325°F (165°C, or gas mark 3). Scoop out tablespoons of dough and roll into small balls by transferring between two spoons. Place them on ungreased baking sheets about 2 inches (5 cm) apart. You should be able to make about 25 balls.

Bake the cookies for 20 to 25 minutes, until the edges of the cookies are starting to brown. If you're making these to use for a crust for a pie or cake, bake them for an additional 5 to 8 minutes, until all but the very tops of the cookies are browned. Let cool on wire racks.

CHOCOLATE MOUSSE CHEESECAKE WITH CHOCOLATE STOUT COOKIE CRUST

Who doesn't love cheesecake? That may read as a rhetorical question, but seriously, I want to know. This cheese-cake uses chocolate, and the Chocolate Stout Cookies from page 137, for a dessert that will make anyone swoon. Cheesecake can be intimidating, but once you learn the Zen of the art of cheesecake baking and practice patience, you will succeed. The secret is letting the cheesecake chill for more than 8 hours. Trust me, it will be well worth the wait.

SERVES 8

FOR COOKIE CRUST:
16 Chocolate Stout Cookies (page 137)

6 tablespoons (85 g) butter, melted

FOR CHEESECAKE:
¾ cup (131 g) chopped dark chocolate

2 pounds (905 g) cream cheese, softened

1 ½ cups (300 g) sugar

¼ teaspoon vanilla bean powder

4 large eggs

1 cup (235 ml) heavy cream

Crumbled Chocolate Stout Cookies (page 137), for serving

Simple Chocolate Sauce (page 94), for serving

To make the cookie crust: Break the cookies in half, put them in a food processor, and blend until they have turned into crumbs. Add the melted butter and pulse until evenly mixed.

Scrape the mixture into the bottom of a 9-inch (23 cm) springform pan. Press the mixture evenly across the bottom of the pan, and put the pan in the refrigerator to let the crust firm up.

To make the cheesecake: Preheat the oven to 300°F (150°C, or gas mark 2). Put the chocolate in the top of a double boiler over medium heat and stir until melted.

Put the cream cheese, sugar, and vanilla powder in a large bowl and pour in the melted chocolate. Whisk by hand or with a handheld mixer until the ingredients have fully combined and the chocolate has cooled. Add the eggs and mix to fully incorporate.

In a separate bowl, whip the heavy cream until it forms soft peaks. Gently fold the softly whipped cream into the chocolate–cream cheese mixture.

Pour the batter into the cookie crust and spread it out evenly. Wrap the springform pan about halfway up the sides tightly with aluminum foil. Fill a large roasting pan about halfway up with water. Put the filled springform pan in the water bath and transfer to the oven. Bake for 65 minutes.

Now for two tips that are really important: 1) Refrain from opening the oven door, because any shift in temperature and oxygen level can cause the cheesecake to crack. 2) When the 65 minutes are up, turn off the oven and crack open the door about 6 inches (15 cm). Leave the cheesecake in the oven as the oven cools down, about 30 minutes.

Remove the cheesecake from the oven and run a knife along the side of the pan to separate the cake from the edges. Place the cheesecake, springform pan and all, in the refrigerator to chill for 8 to 10 hours before serving. Just before removing the cake from the springform pan, sprinkle cookie crumbs on top and drizzle chocolate sauce over them to make an ooey-gooey chocolaty topping.

GUAJILLO CHILE FLAN

Guajillo chiles are a popular everyday chile in and around Mexico City. They're used in sauces and soups and to flavor roasted and stewed meats. They have a very mild heat, but are rich in the beautiful flavor of lightly smoked raisins or prunes. This fruity complexity makes them fun and easy to incorporate into desserts.

SERVES 8

1 ½ cups (300 g) sugar, divided

⅓ cup (80 ml) water

2 cups (475 ml) whole milk

1 cup (235 ml) heavy cream

½ cup (25 g) stemmed and chopped dried guajillo chiles

1 cinnamon stick

10 ounces (280 g) chocolate, chopped

5 large eggs, plus 1 large egg yolk

¼ teaspoon vanilla bean powder

¼ teaspoon salt

NOTE:

Be quick and deliberate when you do this, but also be careful. Sugar burns are among the worst types of burns.

Preheat the oven to 325°F (165°C, or gas mark 3).

Combine ¾ cup (150 g) of the sugar and the water in a small saucepan, preferably a copper one but any will work, over medium-high heat. Stir until the sugar has dissolved. Hold a candy thermometer or meat thermometer in the pan and let the sugar and water cook to about 240°F (116°C) or until a bubbly, copper brown color.

Immediately pour the caramel into a 9-inch (23 cm) pie plate and swirl the plate around until the caramel coats the entire bottom. See note below.

Put the milk, cream, chiles, and cinnamon in the top of a double boiler over medium-low heat. Allow the cinnamon and chiles to steep in the warm milk for 10 to 15 minutes. Make sure the milk never gets above a light simmer.

Strain the milk to remove the solids, and pour the milk back into the double boiler. Whisk the chocolate into the milk until melted and smooth.

Whisk the remaining ¾ cup (150 g) sugar with the eggs, egg yolk, vanilla powder, and salt in a large bowl. Pour into the chocolate-milk mixture and whisk until smooth. Pour the custard mixture into the pie plate.

Place the pie plate into a roasting pan and place in the oven. Carefully add water to the roasting pan to come halfway up the sides of the pie plate. Bake the flan for 30 minutes, or until set but still jiggly.

Remove from the oven, remove the pie plate from the water bath, and let cool on a wire rack for up to 30 minutes. Put in the refrigerator to set for 4 hours. When the flan appears to be fully set, run a thin knife along the sides of the pan to release the flan. Place a plate upside-down on top of the pie plate, hold tightly, and flip it over to release the flan.

LAVENDER CHOCOLATE ICE CREAM

This recipe is courtesy of my dear friends Ryan and Cassi Berk, the proprietors of à la minute, an ice cream shop based in Redlands, California, and with locations all around Southern California. Ryan and I collaborate regularly on sourcing cocoa beans, and on chocolate-related food experiments. Ryan and Cassi are pioneers in the liquid nitrogen ice cream world. Their approach is unique from a lot of the showier brands you'll find. A la minute's focus is on local and seasonal ingredients as the basis for all of their ice cream flavors. When Ryan and Cassi couldn't find a local chocolate company to buy from, they decided to start their own, Parliament Chocolate, so they could sell local chocolate to themselves. This recipe is one of their signatures. Serve with blueberry or raspberry compote, or with Simple Chocolate Sauce (page 94).

SERVES 8

FOR CUSTARD BASE:

5 cups (1.2 L) heavy cream

1½ cups (355 ml) whole milk

9 large egg yolks, whisked

1¾ cups (350 g) sugar

½ teaspoon sea salt

FOR LAVENDER SIMPLE SYRUP:

⅓ cup (69 g) sugar

⅓ cup (80 ml) water

2 tablespoons (11 g) dried culinary lavender

FOR ICE CREAM:

8 cups (1.9 L) custard mix

1 pound (455 g) chocolate, chopped

¼ cup (60 ml) lavender simple syrup

To make the custard base: Combine the cream and milk in a medium saucepan over medium heat and bring to 160°F (71°C).

Turn off the heat and slowly stir in the egg yolks, followed by the sugar and salt. Stir until smooth and fully incorporated.

Strain the mixture through a fine-mesh strainer to ensure you remove any undissolved sugar or salt crystals.

To make the lavender simple syrup: Put the sugar and water in a small saucepan over medium heat. Bring to a simmer, and simmer until the sugar is fully dissolved in the water.

Reduce the heat to low, and add the lavender. Cover and simmer for 30 minutes. Strain the syrup to remove the lavender leaves. Set the syrup aside to cool.

To make the ice cream: Put a double boiler over low heat and give the top pot a few minutes to warm up. Pour 4 cups (950 ml) of the custard mixture into the double boiler. Slowly add the chocolate and stir until melted. Be careful not to let the mixture rise above 110°F (43°C). Add the rest of the custard mixture and the simple syrup. Remove from the heat.

Using a handheld mixer or an immersion blender, blend the mixture for about 30 seconds. Transfer to a bowl, cover, and allow to rest and "cure" in the refrigerator for 12 to 24 hours.

Remove from the refrigerator and mix gently with a spatula. Cover again and put in the freezer for 2 hours.

Remove from the freezer. Some ice crystals may have begun to form. Use a handheld mixer to beat the mixture and break up the ice crystals. Repeat the freezing and beating steps again.

Transfer to an airtight container and put in the freezer overnight to allow the ice cream to harden before serving.

CHOCOLATE-DIPPED PECAN SHORTBREAD HEARTS

These cookies, one of my Mom's classics, are great for any holiday, birthday, special dinner, or work event. The light, sandy, shortbread dough is a perfect complement to great chocolate. These shortbreads were always a staple for both Christmas and Valentine's Day in my family. I hope you enjoy them as much as I do.

MAKES 15 TO 18 COOKIES

1 cup (225 g) butter, softened

½ cup (60 g) confectioners' sugar, plus more for rolling

1¾ cups (220 g) unbleached all-purpose flour, plus more for rolling

¼ teaspoon salt

¼ teaspoon baking powder

⅓ cup (40 g) ground pecans

8 ounces (225 g) dark chocolate, tempered (see page 84)

Preheat the oven to 350°F (180°C, or gas mark 4).

Cream the butter and sugar together until smooth. Combine the flour, salt, baking powder, and ground pecans in a bowl, and stir with the butter-sugar mixture until combined.

Sprinkle a clean work surface with generous equal amounts of flour and confectioners' sugar. Divide the dough into thirds. Flatten each portion under waxed paper dusted with flour and sugar. Roll out the first batch with a rolling pin to between ⅛ and ¼ inch (3 and 6 mm) thick. Remove the waxed paper. Use a heart-shaped cookie cutter measuring about 3¼ inches (8 cm) to cut out cookies.

Place on an ungreased baking sheet and bake for 12 to 14 minutes, until lightly browned around the edges. Watch closely to prevent overbrowning. Repeat the rolling, cutting, and baking with the two remaining batches of dough. Allow the cookies to cool on a wire rack.

Put half the tempered chocolate in a double boiler over medium heat, stir, and allow to fully melt. Turn off the heat, and stir in the other half of the chocolate until fully melted.

Line a baking sheet with parchment or waxed paper. Dip one half of each cookie heart into the melted chocolate and place on the baking sheet to set. Chill the cookies in the freezer for 3 to 5 minutes to set the chocolate.

BLACK SESAME AND COCOA NIB TOFFEE

If there's one thing I like almost as much as making chocolate, it's cooking sugar. There's so much you can do with heat and moisture to alter the chemical makeup of sugar. I won't pretend to fully understand it; I just know it's awesome. Toffee is so much fun to make for a variety of reasons: 1) It will make your kitchen smell awesome. 2) It looks like something totally foreign when it really gets cooking. 3) When you do it right, it's not only delicious, but also feels like a real accomplishment that you took common ingredients like butter, sugar, and water and changed them chemically into something completely new. Consistent and even heat distribution is essential when cooking sugar to prevent unwanted crystallization. I would strongly suggest picking up a small copper pot if you're serious about experimenting with sugar cooking beyond the occasional recipe or two. You will need a candy thermometer or sturdy meat thermometer to execute this recipe. The black sesame seeds and cocoa nibs add interesting flavors and lovely textures.

MAKES ABOUT 16 PIECES

2 cups (455 g) butter

2 cups (455 g) sugar

¼ cup (60 ml) water

¾ teaspoon salt

1½ tablespoons (6 g) cocoa nibs

1 teaspoon black sesame seeds

10 ounces (280 g) chocolate, tempered (see page 84)

Combine the butter, sugar, water, and salt in a 1½- to 2-quart (1.1 to 1.9 L) saucepan (preferably copper). The size of the pan is really important here. The mixture needs room to bubble up, but not so much that it cooks too quickly and burns in spots.

Cook over medium-high heat while stirring constantly with a wooden spoon until the mixture reaches 300°F (150°C), the hard crack stage. When you reach this temperature, your mixture should be a bubbly, dancing substance with an opaque golden brown color. If you get into the mid 200 degrees and your substance is showing signs of separation, see Troubleshooting at right.

Once you reach the proper temperature, remove the pot from the heat and continue to stir. While stirring, add the sesame seeds and cocoa nibs. Once they're mixed in, immediately dump the mixture onto an ungreased baking sheet and spread it around by tilting the pan back and forth. Speed is pretty important here, so make sure you have everything laid out and ready to go. Set aside and allow the toffee to cool.

Put half of the tempered chocolate in a double boiler over medium heat, stir, and allow to fully melt. Turn off the heat, and stir in the other half of the chocolate until fully melted.

Place a piece of parchment or waxed paper on a baking sheet. Break the toffee into whatever size pieces you desire and dip them in the chocolate, coating about half of each piece. Place the toffee on the lined baking sheet to set. Sprinkle additional nibs and/or sesame seeds over the top of the chocolate-coated toffee.

TROUBLESHOOTING NOTE:

If your mixture separates somewhere between 230°F and 260°F (110°C and 127°C) or has not bonded together, take the pot off the heat and add about a tablespoon of water. Stir and allow to cool to 200°F (93°C). Put the pot back on the heat and heat to 300°F (150°C). The additional water should help stabilize your mixture.

EARL GREY CHOCOLATE POUND CAKE

This fabulous recipe comes to us courtesy of David Crofton and Dawn Castle, the owners of One Girl Cookies, an awesome bakery in Brooklyn. This recipe is based on one we dreamt up together for a November tea party we held at the Raaka chocolate factory. We made an Earl Grey–infused chocolate for David and Dawn so they could use it in a pound cake. I gave the pound cake to a bunch of family members for Thanksgiving, and everyone enjoyed it so much that it sparked a bit of a competition to see if anyone could re-create the recipe for David and Dawn's cake. Needless to say, no one could quite match the excellence of their recipe, but now we don't have to. Here is the recipe straight from David himself.

MAKES 1 POUND CAKE

2 cups (250 g) unbleached all-purpose flour

2 teaspoons baking powder

1 teaspoon Earl Grey tea

¾ teaspoon salt

¾ cup (167 g) unsalted butter, softened

1 ¼ cups (250 g) sugar

3 large eggs

1 teaspoon vanilla extract

Zest of 1 orange

¾ cup (165 g) sour cream

1 cup (175 g) chopped dark chocolate

Preheat the oven to 350°F (180°C, or gas mark 4). Spray a 9-inch (23 cm) loaf pan with cooking spray and line the bottom with a rectangle of parchment paper.

Whisk the flour, baking powder, tea, and salt in a large bowl to combine.

In the bowl of a stand mixer, combine the butter and sugar and mix on medium speed for 3 to 5 minutes, until light and fluffy. Lower the mixer speed to low and add the eggs one at a time until combined, followed by the vanilla and orange zest. Mix for 2 to 3 minutes, until fully combined.

With the mixer on low speed, add about one-third of the flour mixture and then scoop in about half of the sour cream. Mix for 10 seconds. Add another third of the flour mixture to the mixer bowl and scoop in the rest of the sour cream. Mix for 10 seconds. Briefly scrape down the mixing bowl and paddle. Add the remaining flour mixture and the chocolate, mixing only until the flour has been incorporated into the batter. Pour the batter into the prepared loaf pan.

Bake for 30 minutes. Rotate the pan in the oven and bake for 25 to 30 minutes longer. Test with a toothpick or cake tester. If the tester comes out clean or with only a few crumbs clinging, the cake is done.

Set the pan on a wire rack to cool. When the pan is cool enough to handle, gently invert the pan onto the cooling rack to remove the cake. Peel off the parchment and let the cake cool completely.

ACKNOWLEDGEMENTS

A monumental thanks to my amazing wife, Catherine, without whom this book wouldn't exist. Thanks for being my inspiration, my rock, my coach, and my recipe-testing (and tasting) hero. Thanks to Mike for embarking on this new journey with me and pushing himself and me to learn new skills. Thanks to Mark for being a friend, role model, and big believer in Raaka and craft chocolate. A big thanks to William Mullan for being a secondary creative force behind this project. A special thanks to Hector, Julie, Tim, Amy, Steve, and Chuck. You guys know who you are and how you've contributed to this book. Thanks to Ryan and Cassi, and Matt and Elaine for being amazing collaborators and true friends. Thanks to the friends and collaborators in the chocolate community that I have all over the world that I have shared so many wonderful times and learned so much from; there are too many of you to list. Thanks to my parents, Mike and Amy, and my brothers, Tim and Josh, for always being supportive and for allowing me to express myself in whatever strange way I was feeling at the moment. Thanks to my mother-in-law, Rita, for her unending and sincere enthusiasm and support. A humble and gracious thanks to my countless personal friends who have helped wrap my chocolate bars, tasted my questionable experiments, and always traveled two blocks past the two blocks I said it'd take to get there. Thanks to John and Jonathan at Quarto for this opportunity and their incredible patience with me. Thanks to John Nanci for teaching a generation how to make chocolate. Thanks to Dawn and David for contributing to this book and being passionate champions of Brooklyn artisan sweets. And last, but certainly not least, thanks to Ryan Cheney and the team at Raaka (members past and present), Orissa, Livingston, Peter, Bryan, Will, Robert, Victoria, Sophie, Eric, Katie, Corinne, Brielle, Graig, Priscilla, Allie, Jim, Tim, and Mad Dog for being a constant source of motivation and people—I can honestly say—I've learned so much from over the years.

ABOUT THE AUTHOR

Nathan Hodge is a Red Hook, Brooklyn–based chocolate maker and entrepreneur. Nathan cofounded Raaka Chocolate in 2010 with Ryan Cheney. The two have watched Raaka grow from humble beginnings in an apartment and shared kitchen space to a nationally acclaimed and recognized brand. Nathan has been featured on Martha Bakes, Unique Sweets, and The Untitled Action Bronson Show, as well as being quoted in the *New York Times,* Crain's, and *The Observer.* Nathan is an avid home cook and seasoned traveler. When he is not out traveling the globe and making friends as an ambassador for Raaka, he is most likely cooking with new and exotic ingredients with his wife Catherine or trying out an obscure restaurant in the far corners of New York's outerboroughs with friends. Nathan has a degree in speech communication from Ithaca College and spent his formative years exploring the cities of Boston and Chicago, where he was born. The upcoming documentary film *Setting the Bar* follows Nathan on a journey to the upper Amazon, in Peru, where he is part of efforts to catalog and preserve ancient varieties of cacao. Nathan's main creative outlet, Raaka's First Nibs, remains the gold standard for innovation in bean-to-bar chocolate. Every year Nathan and his team test and release twenty-four brand new chocolate bars for their subscribers based on international cuisines, new processes, or new origins.

ABOUT THE PHOTOGRAPHER

Mike Grippi is an editorial photographer based in Brooklyn, New York. With a passion for storytelling, Mike uses a camera to explore and engage with people, places, and cultures near and far. To see more of Mike's work, visit www.mikegrippi.com.

INDEX